"Having passed the the last thing I needed was a car that didn't."

Fingers crossed, you'll soon be shedding those L-plates and heading for the open road.

All you need now is a car.

What you don't need is to waste your savings on some sad wreck that will keep letting you down.

Investing in a reliable car will save you money in the long term.

The trouble is it will require some outlay in the short term.

Which is where the Lloyds Bank Personal Loan comes in.

We can lend you what you need, at attractive rates of interest.*

Moreover we'll tailor the loan to suit you, by working out together exactly what your commitments are and how much you can comfortably afford to pay back each month.

With cash in hand, you may even drive away with a bargain.

For further information phone us free on 0800 444210, or call into a Lloyds Bank branch and ask for our brochure.

PERSONAL LOANS

Lloyds Bank

THE THOROUGHBRED BANK.

ACKNOWLEDGEMENTS

I thank my friends most sincerely for the time and patience needed to arrange the contents of the photographs in this book.

A special thank you to the Hertfordshire Constabulary and Thames Valley Police for their assistance; without it, some of the pictures could not have been taken.

Slides developed and printed by Kenton Photographic Colour Laboratories Ltd (Tel: 081-206 0226).

All photographs taken by the author using Leica cameras and lenses.

Other driving titles by Gordon Cole include:

THE MOTORCYCLE TEST MANUAL
DRIVE AND SURVIVE *also published by Kogan Page*

and

SAFER MOTORWAY DRIVING
ADVANCED DRIVING
PASS THE DRIVING TEST
TAKE YOUR CAR ABROAD *all published by Ian Allan Ltd*

All available from good bookshops

The text of *The Highway Code* has been reproduced in this book with the kind permission of the Controller of Her Majesty's Stationery Office. HMSO would like to make clear that *The Illustrated Highway Code* is not a substitute for the official publication *The Highway Code* and that learner drivers will need to study *The Highway Code* itself before taking their test.

THE ILLUSTRATED HIGHWAY CODE

Gordon Cole

KOGAN
PAGE

First published in 1991
incorporating The Highway Code
© Crown copyright 1987

Kogan Page Limited
120 Pentonville Road
London N1 9JN

British Library Cataloguing in Publication Data

A CIP record for this book is available from the British Library.

ISBN 0 7494 0139 7

Typeset by
DP Photosetting, Aylesbury, Bucks
Colour and black & white origination by
Spectrum Reproductions Ltd,
Colchester, Essex
Printed and bound in Great Britain by
Clays Ltd, St Ives plc

This Code, between pages 5 and 47, is issued with the Authority of Parliament (laid before both Houses of Parliament June 1986).

A failure on the part of a person to observe a provision of the Highway Code shall not of itself render that person liable to criminal proceedings of any kind, but any such failure may in any proceedings (whether civil or criminal and including proceedings for an offence under the Traffic Acts, the Public Passenger Vehicles Act 1981 or Sections 18 to 23 of the Transport Act 1985) be relied upon by any party to the proceedings as tending to establish or negative any liability which is in question in those proceedings.
Road Traffic Act 1988, Section 38

CONTENTS

GENERAL

1

Where there is a pavement or footpath, use it. Do not walk next to the kerb with your back to the traffic. Look both ways before you step into the road.

Always walk on the pavement or footpath.

Before you try crossing the road, look both ways.

The road user on foot

2

Where there is no footpath, walk on the right-hand side of the road – it is safer to walk on the side facing oncoming traffic. Keep as close as possible to the side of the road. Take care at right-hand bends. Keep one behind the other if possible, particularly in heavy traffic or in poor light.

3

Do not allow children – up to age five at least – out alone on the road. Go with them, walk between them and the traffic and always keep tight hold of their hands; if you cannot do this, then use reins or secure them firmly in a pushchair. Do not let them run into the road.

Young children must always be accompanied when out on the road.

Keep them restrained or secured so that they are in no danger from passing traffic.

4

Always wear or carry something light-coloured or bright or reflective in the dark or poor light. This is especially important on roads without footpaths. (Reflective material can be seen in headlights at up to three times the distance when compared with ordinary clothes; fluorescent material is highly conspicuous in daylight and at dusk but is of little use in the dark.)

5

A group of people marching on the road should keep to the left. There should be look-outs in front and at the back wearing reflective clothing at night and fluorescent clothing by day. At night the look-out in front should carry a white light, and the one at the back should carry a bright red light visible from the rear. Additional lights should be carried and reflective clothing worn by the outside rank of long columns.

6

You must not walk on motorways or their slip roads to thumb lifts or for any other purpose (see Rule 154).

Reflective material shows up best in the dark.

A group of people marching on the road should keep to the left.

No pedestrians on motorways or their slip roads.

CROSSING THE ROAD

The Green Cross Code
7

The Green Cross Code is a guide for all pedestrians. However, children need to be taught how to use it and should not be allowed out alone until they can understand and apply it. The age at which they can do this will vary: for instance, many children under seven cannot fully understand and apply those parts of the Code requiring judgement of the speed and distance of approaching vehicles. Teaching children the Code and the age at which parents allow them to go out and cross roads by themselves must therefore be suited to each individual child.

All children should learn *The Green Cross Code*.   Traffic islands provide a safe place to cross.

1 First find a safe place to cross, then stop.

It is safer to cross at subways, footbridges, islands, Zebra and Pelican crossings, traffic lights or where there is a policeman, a 'lollipop' man or a traffic warden. If you can't find any good crossing places like these, choose a place where you can see clearly along the roads in all directions. Don't try to cross between parked cars. Move to a clear space and always give drivers a chance to see you clearly.

Always use Zebra and Pelican crossings where you can.

Traffic lights are another safe place to cross.

A 'lollipop' man or woman provides a very safe crossing place for young children.

2 Stand on the pavement near the kerb.

Don't stand too near the edge of the pavement. Stop a little way back from the kerb – where you'll be away from traffic, but where you can still see if anything is coming. If there is no pavement, stand back from the edge of the road but where you can still see traffic coming.

If you can't find any good crossing places like those already mentioned and shown, find a place where you can see clearly along the roads in every direction.

Never try to cross between parked cars, as drivers cannot see you emerging.

If there is no pavement, stand back from the edge of the road.

3 Look all round for traffic and listen.

Traffic may be coming from all directions, so take care to look along every road. And listen, too, because you can sometimes hear traffic before you can see it.

4 If traffic is coming, let it pass. Look all round again.

If there's any traffic near, let it go past. Then look round again and listen to make sure no other traffic is coming.

5 When there is no traffic near, walk straight across the road.

6 Keep looking and listening for traffic while you cross.

Look all round for traffic and listen.

When there is no traffic near it's safe to cross. If there is something in the distance do not cross unless you're *certain* there's plenty of time. Remember, even if traffic is a long way off, it may be coming very fast.

When it's safe, walk straight across the road – don't run.

Once you're in the road, keep looking and listening in case you didn't see some traffic – or in case other traffic suddenly appears.

Crossing where there is an island in the road

8

Use the Green Cross Code (see Rule 7) to cross to the island. Stop there and use the Code again to cross the second half of the road.

Crossing at a junction

9

When you cross at a road junction look out for traffic turning the corner, especially from behind you.

Crossing at a Zebra crossing

10

If there is a Zebra crossing near, always use it. It is very dangerous to cross the road a short distance away from a Zebra crossing. The most dangerous area is usually marked with zigzag lines – don't cross on them.

Use *The Green Cross Code* to cross to the island.

Stop there. Then use the code again to cross the second half of the road.

11

Always give drivers, motorcyclists and pedal cyclists plenty of time to see you and to slow down and stop before you start to cross. If necessary put one foot on the crossing. Until you have stepped on to a Zebra crossing, the traffic does not have to stop for you. Vehicles need more time to stop if the road is slippery because of rain or ice.

12

When the traffic has stopped, walk across but keep looking both ways and listening in case a driver, motorcyclist or pedal cyclist has not seen you and tries to overtake a vehicle which has stopped.

13

If there is an island in the middle of a crossing, pause on it and obey Rules 11 and 12 before crossing the second half of the road – it is a separate crossing.

You do not have right of way until you have stepped on the crossing.

When the traffic has stopped, walk across.

Pause on the island before proceeding.

Crossing at a Pelican crossing

14

Always use a Pelican crossing if one is available, even if you have to walk a bit further to do so. At this type of crossing the traffic is controlled by traffic lights and there is a light signal to tell pedestrians when to cross. Never cross in the area marked with zigzag lines.

AT TRAFFIC LIGHTS AND PELICAN CROSSINGS

AT PELICANS ONLY

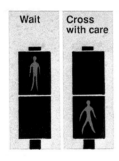

Wait | Cross with care

Do not start to cross

When the red man signal shows, don't cross. Press the button on the box and wait. The lights will soon change and a steady green man signal will appear; you may now cross with care. (At some Pelicans there is also a bleeping sound to tell blind people when the ready green man signal is showing.)
After a short time, the green signal will begin to flash. This means that the lights will soon change again. You should not start to cross but if you have started already you will have time to finish crossing safely.

At Pelicans, light signals tell you when to cross. Never try to cross when the red man is showing.

Do *not* cross a road in the area marked with zigzag lines. Use the crossing available.

When the red man shows, stop, press the button on the box and wait.

Soon a steady green man signal will appear and you may cross.

15

A Pelican which goes straight across the road is one crossing even if there is a central refuge. But if the crossing is staggered (separate crossings one each side of the refuge but not in a straight line) you must press the button on the refuge to get the green man signal for the second crossing.

Although this Pelican has a central refuge it goes straight across the road and is, therefore, one crossing.

This Pelican is staggered and so it is two separate crossings. Therefore, you must press the button on the refuge to get the green man signal for the second crossing.

Crossing at traffic lights
16

If there are pedestrian signals, obey them. If not, watch both the lights and the traffic and do not cross when the lights allow traffic to go forward, even if you think you have time. When the lights are red remember to look out for turning traffic, and remember also that some traffic lights allow traffic to proceed in some lanes while other lanes are stopped.

You must obey pedestrian signals wherever they appear.

Always watch both the lights and the traffic and never cross when the lights allow traffic to go forward, even if you think you have time. This man is foolishly breaking *The Highway Code*.

Always remember to watch out for turning traffic when the lights are red.

Be extra careful at those traffic lights which allow traffic to proceed in some lanes while other lanes are stopped.

Crossings controlled by police, traffic wardens or school crossing patrols
17

When a policeman, traffic warden or school crossing patrol is controlling the traffic, cross the road only when the officer has signalled you to do so. Always cross in front of him.

Cross in front of the officer.

Where there is a gap in the guard rail, you may cross.

Guard rails
18

Where there are guard rails, cross the road only at the gaps provided for pedestrians. Do not climb over the guard rails or walk outside them.

Crossing one-way streets
19

Use the Green Cross Code. Check which way the traffic is going and remember that in one-way streets there will usually be more than one lane of traffic going in the same direction. Do not cross until it is safe to cross all the lanes of traffic.

Guard rails are there for a purpose. Do *not* climb over them.

Do not cross until *all* traffic lanes are clear.

Crossing bus and cycle lanes
20

Use the Green Cross Code. Vehicles in bus lanes may be going faster than traffic in other lanes and in the opposite direction. Watch for cyclists who may be travelling in bus or cycle lanes.

Watch out for vehicles in bus lanes.

When you are forced to cross between parked vehicles, stop where you can be seen and where you can look all round for traffic.

Parked vehicles
21

Try not to cross the road where there are parked vehicles. If you have to cross between parked vehicles, stop at the outside edge of the vehicles where you can be seen by drivers, motorcyclists and pedal cyclists and where you can look all round for traffic. Then continue using the Green Cross Code. Do not stand behind or in front of any vehicle which has its engine running. It might run into you.

Continue to use the Green Cross Code.

Never stand behind or in front of any vehicle which has its engine running. This little girl is in danger of being crushed.

Crossing the road at night
22

Use the Green Cross Code. If there is no convenient pedestrian crossing or island, cross near a street light where you can be seen more easily. Remember that it is more difficult for drivers to see you at night or in poor light, so when visibility is poor, wear something light-coloured or bright. Fluorescent materials help in daylight, reflective in the dark.

When you cannot use a pedestrian crossing or island, cross near a street light which helps drivers to see you.

Always use the Green Cross Code, especially at night.

EMERGENCY VEHICLES

23

Keep out of the road if you see or hear ambulances, fire engines, police or other emergency vehicles with their blue lamps flashing, or their bells, two-tone horns or sirens sounding.

Emergency vehicles have top priority – keep out of their way.

GETTING ON OR OFF A BUS

24

Do not get on or off a bus unless it is standing at a bus stop. If you want to get on a bus at a request stop, give a clear signal for the bus to stop and do not try to get on until it has done so. Never cross behind or in front of a bus. Wait until it has moved off and you have a clear view of the road in both directions.

You must only attempt to board or leave a bus when it is standing at a bus stop.

RAILWAY LEVEL CROSSINGS

25

Take particular care at level crossings (see Rules 186–198).

Never try to cross behind or in front of a bus. It obscures your view of approaching traffic as well as the traffic's view of you.

Wait until the bus has moved off and you can see clearly in both directions. Now you can judge whether or not it is safe to cross.

GENERAL

26

Keep your vehicle in good condition. Pay particular attention to lights, brakes, steering, tyres (including spare), seat belts, demisters, windscreen wipers and washers. Keep windscreens, windows, lights, direction indicators, reflectors, mirrors and number plates clean and clear. Do not drive with a defective or unsuitable exhaust system. If L-plates have been fitted, remove (or cover) them when the vehicle is not being used for driving instruction or practice.

Keep all parts of your vehicle in good condition, including the engine.

All of your lights, windows (including windscreen), direction indicators, reflectors, mirrors and number plates must be kept clean and clear at all times.

27

You must ensure that any loads carried or towed are secure, and do not project unsafely. Do not overload your vehicle or trailer.

If you are using L-plates on your car, remove (or cover) them when you are not using the vehicle for driving instruction or practice.

Ensure any loads carried are safe.

The road user on wheels

28

When on a motorcycle, scooter or moped, you must wear a safety helmet of approved design which must be fastened securely. You should also wear sturdy boots and gloves. To help others to see you, wear something light-coloured or bright. Reflective materials help in the dark; fluorescent materials help in daylight, as do dipped headlights on larger machines (over 150cc–200cc).

Riders of motorcycles, scooters or mopeds are much more vulnerable than car drivers when on the road. A safety helmet of approved design must be worn and fastened securely.

29

Do not drive if you feel tired or unwell. Fatigue can cause serious accidents.

Tiredness or illness can severely affect your driving ability.

Sturdy boots and gloves should also be worn for safety and protection. Always wear something light-coloured or bright to help others see you, both day and night.

30

Never drive if you are under the influence of drugs or medicines. They can seriously affect your driving ability. Always ask your doctor whether it is safe for you to drive when taking prescribed medicines.

31

If you need spectacles to meet the official eyesight standard, wear them. It is an offence to drive with uncorrected defective vision.

32

Do not use tinted optical equipment of any kind (sun-glasses, night driving spectacles, ski goggles, tinted helmet visors) at night or in conditions of poor visibility.

33

Tinted glass does not help your vision. Do not use spray-on or other tinting materials for windows and windscreens.

If you need glasses, you *must* wear them when driving.

This tinted visor should not be worn in poor visibility.

The quality of vision from this car would be greatly impaired, especially at night or in poor light.

ALCOHOL AND THE ROAD USER

34

Drinking alcohol seriously affects driving ability. It reduces co-ordination, increases reaction time and impairs judgement of speed, distance and risk while inspiring a false sense of confidence. The risk of an accident increases sharply for drivers above the legal limit of 35 microgrammes of alcohol per 100 millilitres of breath. The driving of many people who feel perfectly sober is seriously affected well below this limit.

About one third of all drivers, motorcyclists and pedestrians who are killed in road accidents have alcohol levels above the legal limit for driving.

Driving above the legal limit means losing your licence for a long period and can mean a heavy fine or imprisonment. The safest course is not to drink and drive.

You may *feel* fine, but even one small alcoholic drink *will impair* your driving ability to some degree.

SEAT BELTS

35

If you are involved in an accident, wearing a seat belt halves the risk of death or serious injury. Drivers and front seat passengers in most vehicles must wear a seat belt. Those exempt from the law include holders of a medical exemption certificate, drivers carrying out a manoeuvre which includes reversing, and those engaged in making local rounds of deliveries and collections in a vehicle constructed or adapted for that purpose. It is your responsibility to wear the belt unless exempt. Make sure your seat belts are properly adjusted and that your passengers know how to use them.

If you are driving or you are a front seat passenger, you must always wear a seat belt, unless you are exempt.

36

The driver is responsible in law for ensuring that children under 14 are suitably restrained when they are travelling in the front and rear. In the front a child under one year must use an approved child restraint designed for its age and weight. A child over one may wear any approved child restraint or an adult seat belt. In the rear a child must be restrained if an appropriate restraint is fitted and

People who make local rounds of deliveries and collections in a vehicle used especially for that purpose are exempt from wearing a seat belt while doing so.

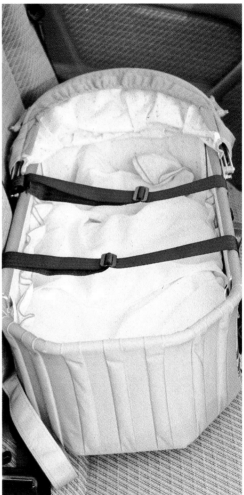

For infants less than a year old, an infant carrier or carry cot should be used and firmly secured with straps.

available to use. The term 'appropriate restraint' includes the following:

Infants under 1 year old – an infant carrier or a carry cot which is held by straps.

Children aged 1, 2 or 3 years – an appropriate child seat or harness or booster cushion with adult belt. (Not a household cushion.)

Children from 4 to 14 years old – an appropriate child seat or harness or an adult belt, with or without a booster cushion.

In the rear an adult may be restrained in preference to a child. However an adult must not deny a child the use of a restraint by sitting in a seat and not using the restraint.

When carrying children aged 1, 2 or 3 years, a child seat or harness should be used, or a booster cushion with adult belt.

For children between 4 and 14 years old, a child seat, harness or an adult belt should be used, with or without a booster cushion.

37

Do not carry children in the luggage space behind the rear seats of an estate car or hatchback unless the manufacturers have provided seats for this purpose. Ensure that child safety locks on doors, where fitted, are secured when children are being carried.

It is dangerous to carry children in the luggage space of estates or hatchbacks unless proper seats are provided for this.

SIGNS

38

Know your traffic signs and road markings (see pages 128–31) and act on them always.

In this short stretch of road, there are a number of traffic signs and road markings, which you must be able to understand and act on in order to drive safely and legally.

SIGNALS

39

Give signals if they would help or warn other road users. Give only the correct signals – those illustrated on page 127. Give them clearly and in good time. Always be sure that your direction indicator signals are cancelled after a manoeuvre.

Signals are essential in letting other road users know of your intentions.

Make sure you give the correct signals, clearly and in plenty of time.

Always remember to cancel your direction indicator signals after a manoeuvre, as this driver has done after turning into a side road.

While on the road, you must continually be on the look-out for the signals of other drivers.

40

Watch out for the signals of other drivers, motorcyclists or pedal cyclists and take any necessary action promptly.

Be particularly vigilant where motorcyclists or cyclists are involved. Their signals and actions are not always as obvious as those of car drivers.

You must act promptly on any signal given by another road user.

41
You must obey signals given by police officers and traffic wardens directing traffic (see page 126) or signs displayed by school crossing patrols.

All signals given by police officers directing traffic must be obeyed. For example, if a police officer signalled to you in the way shown above, you would have to *stop*.

Here you would have to stop if you were approaching from behind the traffic warden.

Always stop for school crossing patrols.

MOVING OFF

42

Before moving off, always use your mirrors; but look round as well for a final check. Signal if necessary before moving out; move only when you can do so safely without making other road users change speed or direction.

It is essential to use your mirrors to check what is coming along the road behind you *before* you try to move off.

Always check by looking over your shoulder before you move away.

If you need to, signal before moving out. Only move off when you are sure you can do so safely without forcing other road users to change their speed or direction.

DRIVING ALONG

43

Keep to the left, except when road signs or markings indicate otherwise or when you intend to overtake, or turn right, or when you have to pass stationary vehicles or pedestrians in the road. Allow others to overtake you if they want to. You must not drive on a footpath or pavement by the side of the road.

This car is driving in the correct position on the road – to the *left*.

When overtaking, you must move out onto the right-hand side of the road.

When turning right, you must move to just left of the centre line, as shown above.

In order to pass stationary vehicles or pedestrians, you must also move out from the left-hand side of the road.

44

Use your mirrors often so that you know what is behind and to each side of you.

You must be continually aware of what is behind and on either side of you, so keep checking your mirrors at all times.

45

On narrow or winding roads, or where there is a lot of oncoming traffic, drivers of large or slow-moving vehicles should be prepared to pull in, and slow down or stop, as soon as there is a suitable opportunity to do so, to give faster vehicles a chance to overtake.

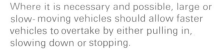

Where it is necessary and possible, large or slow-moving vehicles should allow faster vehicles to overtake by either pulling in, slowing down or stopping.

46

Well before you overtake, or turn left, or turn right, or slow down, or stop, use your mirrors (motorcyclists should always look behind, even if they have mirrors fitted); then give the appropriate signal if necessary.

Remember the routine: **MIRRORS - SIGNAL - MANOEUVRE**.

Check in your mirrors well before you overtake.

Then give the appropriate signal if necessary.

When turning left, always use your mirrors as there could be a cyclist approaching on the inside.

If so, give way to the cyclist and then give the appropriate signal if necessary.

When turning right, always use your mirrors to check what is following behind before you manoeuvre.

Use your mirrors whenever you slow down or stop to check the traffic behind you.

Then give the appropriate signal
if necessary.

In this instance, it is the brake lights.

Before starting any manoeuvre, motorcyclists
should always look behind, even if they have
mirrors fitted. They should then give the
appropriate signal if they need to.

47

Always keep a special look-out for cycles and motor-cycles, particularly when overtaking or turning. Bear in mind that two-wheelers are much less easy to see than larger vehicles and that their riders have the same rights to consideration as other road users and are more vulnerable. Drivers (especially of long vehicles or of vehicles towing trailers) should leave plenty of room for pedal cyclists in particular.

Give pedal cyclists and motorcyclists the same consideration as you would other road users. Keep a special look-out for them and always allow them plenty of room.

48

Driving for long distances may make you feel sleepy. To help prevent this, make sure there is plenty of fresh air in your vehicle. If you become tired on a journey, stop and rest at a suitable parking place.

If you feel tired or at all drowsy on a journey, you must stop and rest at a convenient place, and try to get some fresh air.

49

You must obey the speed limits for the road and for your vehicle. Remember that, except on motorways, there is a 30 mph speed limit on all roads where there are street lights unless signs show otherwise. Bear in mind that any speed limit is a maximum. It does not mean that it is safe to drive at that speed – always take into account all the conditions at the time. (A table of speed limits, according to road and vehicle, is shown on page 125.)

Always keep within the speed limit for the road you are on and for the vehicle you are driving.

Except on motorways, the speed limit is 30 mph on all roads where there are street lights unless signs show otherwise.

Always remember that any speed limit is a maximum and it may not always be safe to drive at that speed. For example, in the situation shown here, it would be very dangerous to drive at 30 mph.

50

Never drive so fast that you cannot stop well within the distance you can see to be clear. Go much more slowly if the road is wet or icy or if there is fog. Drive more slowly at night. Remember – it can be especially difficult to see pedestrians and cyclists at night and in poor daylight conditions. Do not brake sharply except in an emergency.

You must drive at a speed at which you are able to stop well within the distance you can see to be clear ahead of you. Approaching this bend at a high speed would be extremely dangerous.

Never brake sharply except in an emergency.

When road conditions are bad due to the weather, or if visibility is poor, drive much more slowly than you would normally.

51

Leave enough space between you and the vehicle in front so that you can pull up safely if it slows down or stops suddenly. The safe rule is never to get closer than the overall stopping distance shown below. But on the open road, in good conditions, a gap of one metre for each mph of your speed or a two-second time gap may be enough. This will also leave space for an overtaking vehicle to pull in. On wet or icy roads the gap should be at least doubled. Drop back if an overtaking vehicle pulls into the gap in front of you.

Leaving enough space between you and the vehicle in front is especially important on fast roads. On motorways, 'pile-ups' are frequently caused by vehicles travelling too close together at high speed.

Always try to leave one metre for each mph of the speed you are travelling at or a two-second time gap between you and the vehicle in front. This leaves space for an overtaking vehicle to pull in. If an overtaking vehicle pulls in in front of you, drop back to a safe distance behind it.

Shortest stopping distances – in metres and **feet**			
mph	Thinking distance	Braking distance	Overall stopping distance
20	6 **20**	6 **20**	12 **40**
30	9 **30**	14 **45**	23 **75**
40	12 **40**	24 **80**	36 **120**
50	15 **50**	38 **125**	53 **175**
60	18 **60**	55 **180**	73 **240**
70	21 **70**	75 **245**	96 **315**
(See diagram on back cover)			

On a dry road, a good car with good brakes and tyres and an alert driver will stop in the distances shown. Remember these are shortest stopping distances. Stopping distances increase greatly with wet and slippery roads, poor brakes and tyres, and tired drivers.

52

Make way for ambulances, fire engines, police or other emergency vehicles when their blue lamps are flashing or their bells, two-tone horns or sirens are sounding.

53

In town give way to buses indicating an intention to move out from bus stops if you can do so safely.

Always give way to buses indicating to pull away from bus stops in built-up areas.

It is both illegal and dangerous to use a hand-held microphone or portable telephone while you are driving, except in an emergency.

USE OF MICROPHONES AND CAR TELEPHONES

54

Do not use a hand-held microphone or telephone handset while your vehicle is moving, except in an emergency. You should only speak into a fixed, neckslung or clipped-on microphone when it would not distract your attention from the road. Do not stop on the hard shoulder of a motorway to answer or make a call, however urgent.

DRIVING IN FOG

55

When driving in fog:

a Check your mirrors and slow down. Keep a safe distance. You should always be able to pull up within your range of vision.

b Don't hang on to someone else's tail lights; it gives a false sense of security.

c Watch your speed; you may be going much faster than you think. Do not speed up to get away from a vehicle which is too close behind you.

d Remember that if you are driving a heavy vehicle it may take longer to pull up than the vehicle ahead.

e Warning signals are there to help and protect; observe them.

f See and be seen. Use dipped headlamps or front fog lamps. Only use rear fog lamps when visibility is seriously reduced (Rule 120). Use your windscreen wipers and demisters.

g Check and clean windscreens, lights, reflectors and windows whenever you can.

h Remember that fog can drift rapidly and is often patchy. Even if it seems to be clearing, you can suddenly find yourself back in thick fog.

i Take particular care when driving in fog after dark.

j If you must drive in fog, allow more time for your journey.

When travelling in fog, go much more slowly and keep a safe distance from the vehicle in front of you.

Hanging on to someone else's tail light gives you a false sense of security and causes you to drive too near to the vehicle in front.

The most important rule when driving in fog is to see and be seen. Always use dipped headlamps or front fog lamps. Rear fog lamps should only be used when visibility is seriously reduced.

THE SAFETY OF PEDESTRIANS

56

Drive carefully and slowly when pedestrians are about, particularly in crowded shopping streets, when you see a bus stopped, or near a parked milk float or mobile shop. Watch out for pedestrians emerging suddenly, for example from behind parked or stopped vehicles. Remember, pedestrians may have to cross roads where there are no crossings; show them consideration.

When pedestrians are about, drive slowly and carefully keeping a special look-out for any which may emerge suddenly into your path. Always be considerate and allow pedestrians to cross.

57

Two out of three pedestrians killed or seriously injured are either under 15 or over 60. The young and the elderly may not judge speeds very well and may step into the road when you do not expect them. Watch out for blind people who may be carrying white sticks (white with two red reflectorised bands for deaf/blind people) or using guide dogs, and for the disabled or infirm. Give them plenty of time to cross the road. Remember that deaf people may not hear your vehicle approaching.

The young and the elderly are the most vulnerable pedestrians and so are the most common victims of serious or fatal accidents.

Look out particularly for blind people who may be carrying white sticks (white with two red reflectorised bands for deaf and blind people), as they could easily step out in front of you.

Those using guide dogs must also be given special consideration.

Always allow the disabled or infirm plenty of time to cross the road.

58

Drive slowly near schools and look out for children getting on or off buses. Stop when signalled to do so by a school crossing patrol showing a 'STOP – CHILDREN' sign. In places of particular danger, there may be a flashing amber signal below the advance sign which warns of a school crossing patrol operating ahead.

When you are driving near schools reduce your speed and look out for children near the road especially when they are getting on or off buses.

59

Be careful near a parked ice-cream van – children are more interested in ice-cream than in traffic.

Children may well run out into the road near a parked ice-cream van, so drive very carefully.

Sometimes a flashing amber signal below the advance sign will warn you of a school crossing patrol operating ahead. Always stop when signalled to do so at a patrol.

60

When coming to a Zebra crossing, keep a look out for pedestrians waiting to cross (particularly children, the elderly, the infirm and people with prams) and be ready to slow down or stop to let them cross. When anyone has stepped on to a crossing, you must give way. Signal to other drivers that you mean to slow down or stop. Allow more time for stopping on wet or icy roads. Do not signal pedestrians to cross; another vehicle may be approaching.

You must give way once a pedestrian has started to cross.

When you are about to slow down or stop at a crossing, signal your intention to other drivers, as shown above.

61

You must not overtake in the area marked by zigzag lines on the approach to Zebra and Pelican crossings. You must not overtake the moving motor vehicle nearest the crossing, or the leading vehicle which has stopped at a Zebra to give way to a pedestrian on the crossing or at a Pelican to comply with the traffic lights. Even when there are no zigzags never overtake just before a pedestrian crossing.

Always allow more time to stop on wet or icy roads and never signal a pedestrian to cross as another vehicle may be approaching which might not stop.

Never, under any circumstances, must you overtake in the area marked by zigzag lines or just before a Zebra or Pelican crossing.

62

In traffic queues, leave pedestrians crossings clear.

63

At pedestrian crossings controlled by lights, or by a police officer or traffic warden, give way to pedestrians who are still crossing when the signal allows vehicles to move.

64

At Pelican crossings the signals have the same meaning as traffic lights except that a flashing amber signal will follow the red 'STOP' signal. When the amber light is flashing you must give way to any pedestrians on the crossing; otherwise you may proceed. A straight Pelican is one crossing even when there is a central refuge and you must wait for people crossing from the further side of the refuge. Don't harass pedestrians – for instance, by revving your engine.

65

When turning at a road junction, give way to pedestrians who are crossing the road into which you are turning.

66

When entering or emerging from property bordering on a road, give way to pedestrians as well as to traffic on the road. Remember: pavements are for people – not for motor vehicles.

Even at crossings where signals allow vehicles to move, if pedestrians are still crossing you must *give way*.

At Pelicans, a flashing amber light means *give way* to pedestrians on the crossing.

Pedestrians crossing the road into which you are turning have right of way, so *stop* for them.

Always give way to pedestrians on the pavement as well as to traffic on the road, when entering or emerging from any premises at the side of the road.

67

Be careful when there are pedestrians, processions or other marching groups in the road, particularly where there is no footpath. Give them plenty of room. Be especially careful on a left-hand bend and keep your speed down.

ANIMALS

68

Go slowly when driving past animals. Give them plenty of room and be ready to stop if necessary. Do not frighten the animals by sounding your horn or revving your engine. Watch out for animals being led on your side of the road and be especially careful at a left-hand bend.

When pasing by animals, drive slowly and do *not* do anything to frighten them.

SINGLE-TRACK ROADS

69

Some roads (often called single-track roads) are only wide enough for vehicles to move in one direction at a time. They have special passing places. When you see a vehicle coming towards you, or the driver behind you wants to overtake and the passing place is on your side, pull in; if it is on the other side, wait opposite it. Give way to vehicles coming uphill whenever possible. Do not park in passing places.

Use passing places to let oncoming traffic go past or for allowing other vehicles to overtake you.

Never use passing places as pleasant spots to park!

LINES AND LANES ALONG THE ROAD

70

A single broken line, with long markings and short gaps, in the middle of the road is a hazard warning line. Do not cross it unless you can see that the road well ahead is clear.

The car shown here is about to try and cross the hazard warning line. He is endangering himself and other road users by doing so. Always ensure that the road ahead is clear before crossing the hazard line.

It would be very dangerous for this driver to cross the line now.

71

Where there are double white lines along the road and the line nearer to you is solid, you must not cross or straddle it except when you need to get in and out of premises or a side road, or when you are ordered to cross the lines by a policeman or traffic warden, or when you have to avoid a stationary obstruction.

Never cross a solid white line when it is nearer to you except when you need to enter or leave premises or a side road.

The only other occasion on which you may cross a solid white line on your side is when you need to avoid a stationary obstruction or to turn right.

72

Where there are double white lines along the road and the line nearer to you is broken, you may cross the lines to overtake if you can do so safely and before reaching a solid white line on your side. It is up to you to be sure it is safe.

Although there is no oncoming traffic to prevent overtaking here, there would be too little time to do so before you reached the double solid white lines.

The chevrons here separate traffic already on the motorway from traffic approaching the motorway from the slip road.

73

Areas of white diagonal stripes or white chevrons painted on the road are to separate traffic streams liable to be a danger to each other or to protect traffic turning right. Do not drive over these areas if you can avoid doing so. Where the chevron has a solid white edge line you must not enter the area except in an emergency.

These chevrons protect traffic turning right from both the traffic following and from that which is oncoming.

You should always avoid driving over chevrons, and those surrounded by a solid white line (as above) should never be entered except in an emergency.

74

Keep between the traffic lane markings – the short broken white lines which divide the road into lanes. Keep in the left-hand lane unless you are going to overtake, turn right or pass parked vehicles. Coloured reflecting road studs may be used with white lines – white studs mark the lanes or centre of the road, while the edge of the carriageway may have red studs on the left-hand side and amber by the central reservation of dual carriageways. Green studs may be used across lay-bys and side roads.

75

Do not move unnecessarily from lane to lane. If you need to move into another lane, first use your mirrors. If it is safe to move over, signal before doing so. Make sure you will not force another vehicle to swerve or slow down.

76

When coming to junctions, be guided by any lane indication arrows on the road or on signs.

Always drive within lane markings and in the left-hand lane unless you are overtaking, turning right or passing stationary vehicles. Reflective, coloured studs on dual carriageway roads are to help you stay in the correct lane when driving after dark.

Only move from lane to lane when you need to.

The driver of the white car above has obviously not checked his mirrors or signalled his intention to move from one lane into another. Consequently, another vehicle has been forced to slow down. Do not change lanes before you have checked it is *safe* to do so.

Ensure you choose your lane well in advance. Do not swerve from lane to lane.

77

In traffic hold-ups, do not try to 'jump the queue' by cutting into another lane or by overtaking the vehicles waiting in front of you.

78

If a single-carriageway (ie undivided) road has three lanes, use the middle lane only for overtaking and turning right. Remember that you have no more right to use the middle lane than a driver coming from the opposite direction. Do not use the right-hand lane.

79

If a single-carriageway road has four or more lanes do not use the lanes on the right-hand half of the road unless signs and markings indicate that you may do so.

80

On a three-lane dual carriageway you may stay in the middle lane when there are slower vehicles in the left-hand lane, but you should return to the left-hand lane when you have passed them. The right-hand lane is for overtaking (or for right-turning traffic); if you use it for overtaking move back into the middle lane and then into the left-hand lane as soon as you can, but without cutting in.

In situations such as this one, cutting in or overtaking is both inconsiderate and dangerous, and gets you no further in the end.

On this kind of three-lane (but two-way) carriageway, only use the middle lane for overtaking or turning right.

On a four-lane (but two-way) carriageway, do not use the two lanes on the right-hand side of the road unless signs and markings tell you that you may.

On three-lane dual carriageways, you should stay in the left-hand lane, except when overtaking slower vehicles. Always return to that lane when you have passed them.

81

In one-way streets, choose the correct lane for your exit as soon as you can. Never change lanes suddenly. Unless road markings indicate otherwise, choose the left-hand lane when going to the left, the right-hand lane when going to the right and any convenient lane when going straight on. Remember – other vehicles could be passing on both sides.

Select the correct lane for the way you want to go when in a one-way street in good time.

Bus lanes are easily recognised by signs and markings and the restrictions on their use by other vehicles is indicated on special time plates, as shown here.

82

A bus lane, which is shown by signs and road markings, may operate for 24 hours or for other periods shown by time plates. Details of those vehicles which are permitted to use the special lane are indicated on the signs. Outside the indicated period of operation all vehicles may use the bus lane.

The driver of this car is committing an offence by parking in a cycle lane, marked by a solid white line.

Drivers should only enter a cycle lane marked by a broken white line if they cannot avoid doing otherwise.

83

Cycle lanes are shown by signs and road markings. It is an offence to drive or park a motor vehicle in a cycle lane which is marked by a solid white line. Where the cycle lane is marked by a broken white line, drivers should not enter it if they can avoid doing so.

OVERTAKING

84

Do not overtake unless you are sure
you can do so without danger to
others or to yourself. Before you start
to overtake make sure that the road is
clear far enough ahead and behind.
Use your mirrors and if you are on a
motorcycle or pedal cycle look behind
and to your offside. Signal before you
start to move out. Be particularly
careful at dusk, in the dark and in fog
or mist, when it is more difficult to
judge speed and distance.

Before overtaking, always check the road is clear
ahead and behind.

It is equally important to check that the road behind
is clear enough to overtake.

Always use your mirrors *before* you begin the
manoeuvre.

Always signal *before* you start to move out.

Remember: **Mirrors – Signal – Manoeuvre.**

85

On fast roads, vehicles may be coming up behind much more quickly than you think. Make sure that the lane you will be moving into is clear for a long way behind.

86

Once you have started to overtake, move quickly past the vehicle you are overtaking and leave it plenty of room. Then move back to the left side of the road as soon as you can, but without cutting in.

Ensure that the lane you are about to move into is clear for a long way behind. Vehicles approaching from behind may be travelling a lot faster than they seem.

When you are actually overtaking leave the other vehicle plenty of room and move quickly past it.

You must move back to the left as soon as you can.

However, do *not* cut in in front of the vehicle you have passed, as this car is doing. Leave ample room in front as well as to the side.

87

When overtaking motorcycles, pedal cycles or horse riders, give them plenty of room, at least as much as you would a car. Remember that cyclists may be unable to keep a straight course, particularly in windy conditions, or where the road surface is poor. Do not overtake motorcycles, pedal cycles or horse riders immediately before turning left.

Always allow motorcycles, pedal cycles and horse riders plenty of room, as cyclists in particular cannot always steer a steady course.

This driver is acting both inconsiderately and dangerously in overtaking a cyclist immediately before turning left.

88

Overtake only on the right except:

a when the driver in front has signalled that he intends to turn right and you can overtake him on the left without getting in the way of others and without entering a bus lane during its period of operation;

b when you want to turn left at a junction;

c when traffic is moving slowly in queues and vehicles in a lane on the right are moving more slowly than you are;

d in one-way streets (but not dual carriageways) where vehicles may pass on either side.

If there is room for you to do so, you may overtake on the left when the driver in front has signalled that he is going to turn right.

Similarly, when you want to turn left at a junction and another vehicle wants to turn right at the same junction, you may pass him on the left.

In multi-lane traffic queues like this one, you can overtake on the left when traffic in the lanes to your right is moving more slowly than you.

Where vehicles may pass on either side, as in a one-way street (but *not* a dual carriageway), you may also overtaken on the left.

89

When traffic is moving as described at Rule 88c, you may move to a lane on your left only in order to turn left or to park. Do not change lanes to the left in order to overtake. Motorcyclists overtaking traffic queues should look out for pedestrians crossing between vehicles.

90

Do not increase your speed while being overtaken. Slow down, if necessary, to let the overtaking vehicle pass.

91

On the two-lane road, give way to vehicles coming towards you before you pass parked vehicles or other obstructions on the left-hand side of the road.

In multi-lane traffic queues, you may only change lanes to turn left, and *not* to overtake.

Always *give way* to vehicles coming towards you when there are parked vehicles or other obstructions on your side of the road. It is dangerous to try and force your way through.

92

You MUST NOT overtake:

— if you would have to cross or straddle double white lines with a solid line nearer to you;

— if you are within the zigzag area on the approach to a Zebra or Pelican crossing (see Rule 61 for definition);

— after a 'No Overtaking' sign and until the end of the restriction.

Do not overtake:

where you cannot see far enough ahead to be sure it is safe to do so, for example, when at or coming to:

— a corner or bend;
— a hump-backed bridge;
— the brow of a hill; or

where you might come into conflict with other road users, for example,

— at a road junction;
— at a level crossing;
— where the road narrows;
— on the approach to any type of pedestrian crossing;
— where it would involve driving over an area marked with diagonal stripes or chevrons.

Do not overtake:

— when to do so would force another vehicle to swerve or slow down.

IF IN DOUBT – DO NOT OVERTAKE.

Only overtake when you are certain that it is safe and legal to do so. For example, here it is *not* safe on a corner or bend, nor is it legal because of the double solid white lines.

On a hump-backed bridge do *not* overtake; you cannot see what is coming towards you.

Never overtake at or near a road junction. The overtaking vehicle here will have to brake to avoid a collision with the car emerging from the junction.

At a level crossing, overtaking is also extremely dangerous and illegal.

Do not overtake where the road narrows. You may find that you run out of road while overtaking.

Never overtake on the approach to any type of pedestrian crossing. There could be somebody crossing who you cannot see.

Never attempt to overtake when it would force another vehicle to swerve or slow down, as above.

IF IN DOUBT – DO NOT OVERTAKE.

ROAD JUNCTIONS

93

Approach junctions with great care. Consider your road position and your speed. Drive on only when you are sure it is safe to do so and that you will not block the junction. Watch out for long vehicles which may be turning – left or right – at a junction ahead but which may have to use the whole width of the road in order to make the turn. Watch out for pedal cyclists and motorcyclists, and for pedestrians waiting to cross.

Always approach junctions with care, watching both your road position and speed and what can and cannot be seen.

Look out for long vehicles at a junction ahead, which may have to use the whole width of the road in order to turn, as this bus has to.

94

When waiting to emerge at a junction do not assume that a vehicle approaching from the right which is signalling with its left-hand direction indicator *will* turn left. Wait to make sure.

Be wary of pedal cyclists and motorcyclists and pedestrians waiting to cross at junctions.

At the T-junction above, the driver of the car which is emerging is waiting until she is certain that the car which is signalling to turn left, will actually turn left.

95

At a junction with double broken white lines across the road (it may also have a 'Give Way' sign or an inverted triangle on the carriageway) you must be ready to let traffic on the major road go by first.

96

At junctions with a 'STOP' sign and a solid white line across your apprach, you must stop at the line. Wait for a safe gap in the traffic before you move off.

97

When crossing a dual carriageway or turning right into one, treat each half as a separate road. Wait in the central dividing strip (the central reservation) until there is a safe gap in the traffic on the second half of the road. However, where the central reservation is too narrow for the length of your vehicle, you should wait in the side road until you can cross the dual carriageway in one movement.

If it is wide enough, cross to the central reservation and wait. Otherwise, dual carriageways should be treated as one road.

You must *always* STOP at a junction marked with a solid white line and a 'STOP' sign.

98

Where a junction has a mini-roundabout, it will have a sign (as shown on page 128) placed before the 'Give Way' line and Rules 110–115 must be obeyed.

99

Box junctions have criss-cross yellow lines painted on the road. You must not enter the box if your exit road or lane from it is not clear. But you may enter the box when you want to turn right and are prevented from doing so only by oncoming traffic or by vehicles waiting to make a right turn.

Always be prepared to *give way* at a mini-roundabout.

Do *not* enter a box junction if your exit or lane from it is not clear. However, you can enter if you want to turn right but cannot do so because of oncoming traffic, as shown above.

Junctions controlled by police or traffic wardens
100

When all traffic is held up by a police officer or traffic warden, you must not filter to the left or right until he/she signals you to do so.

When stopped by a traffic controller, do *not* filter to the left or right until you are signalled to do so.

Junctions controlled by traffic lights
101
Do not go forward when the traffic lights are green unless there is room for you to clear the junction safely. Never go forward when the red and amber lights are showing together.

102
Where traffic lights have a green arrow filter signal, do not get into the lane where filtering is allowed unless you want to go in the direction shown by the arrow. Give other drivers, especially cyclists, room to move into the correct lane.

103
At junctions controlled by traffic lights, vehicles required to stop must wait behind the solid white 'STOP' line marked across the approach.

When the traffic lights are green do *not* go forward unless there is room for you to clear the junction safely.

When red and amber lights are showing together, *never* proceed.

Filter lanes at traffic lights are for vehicles who want to go in the direction shown by the arrow only. If you want to go in another direction, as shown above, stay in the correct lane.

Vehicles signalled to stop at traffic lights must wait *behind* the solid white 'STOP' line.

104

Cyclists, motorcyclists and pedestrians are particularly at risk at junctions. Look out for them before you turn. Give them room.

TURNING RIGHT

105

Well before you turn right, use your mirrors to make sure you know the position and movement of traffic behind you. When it is safe, give a right turn signal and, as soon as you can do so safely, take up position just left of the middle of the road or in the space marked for right-turning traffic. If you can, leave room for other vehicles to pass on the left. Wait until there is a safe gap between you and any oncoming vehicle; look out for cyclists, motorcycles and pedestrians; then make the turn, but do not cut the corner. Give way to pedestrians crossing the road into which you are turning.

Remember:

Mirrors – Signal – Manoeuvre.

Watch out for pedestrians, cyclists and motorcyclists before you turn at junctions, and give them room to cross or turn.

Use your mirrors to check that you know the position and movement of traffic behind you, well *before* you turn right.

Give a right turn signal when you are sure it is safe to do so.

Then move into the correct position for turning right which is just left of the middle of the road, leaving room for other vehicles to pass on the left, if possible.

Wait in this position until there is a safe gap between you and any oncoming traffic.

Look out for any cyclists, motorcyclists or pedestrians and make sure the road is clear.

Then make the turn, but do *not* cut the corner.

106

When turning right at a junction where there is an oncoming vehicle also turning right, drive your vehicle so that you keep it to your right and pass behind it (offside to offside). Check for other traffic on the carriageway you intend to cross before completing the turn. If the layout of the junction or the traffic situation is such that offside-to-offside passing is impractical, or if nearside-to-nearside passing is indicated either by road markings or by the position of the other vehicle, watch carefully for traffic approaching on the carriageway you intend to cross, which may be masked by the other vehicle.

If you meet a right-turning vehicle at a junction where you are also turning right, pass behind it (offside-to-offside) in order to make your turn, while checking for other oncoming traffic.

Where offside-to-offside is impractical, or nearside-to-nearside passing is indicated by road markings or by the position of the other vehicle, be sure to watch out for any traffic approaching on the carriageway you intend to cross, which may be concealed by the vehicle you are passing.

107

When turning right from a dual carriageway, wait in the opening in the central reservation until you are sure it is safe to cross the other carriageway.

Use the central reservation to wait in (as shown here), until you can see that it is safe to cross the other carriageway.

TURNING LEFT

108

Well before you turn left, use your mirrors and give a left turn signal. Before and after the turn keep as close to the left as safety and the length of your vehicle will allow. Do not overtake a cyclist or motorcyclist immediately before turning left, and always check that one is not coming up behind on your left before turning. Give way to pedestrians crossing the road into which you are turning.

Use your mirrors well before you turn left to check what is behind you.

Then give a left turn signal.

Keep as close to the left as you can, both before and after the turn. Always avoid swinging out when turning.

Never overtake a cyclist or motorcyclist immediately before turning left, and always check in your mirrors that one is not coming up behind on your left before turning.

109

If you intend to turn left across a bus or cycle lane, look out for any vehicles, especially cycles, that may be using it.

ROUNDABOUTS

110

When approaching a roundabout, watch out for traffic already on it. Take special care to look out for cyclists or motorcyclists ahead or to the side. Give way to traffic on your right unless road markings indicate otherwise; but keep moving if the way is clear. At some junctions there may be more than one roundabout. At each, apply the normal rules for roundabouts. Keep a special look out for the 'Give Way' lines.

Before turning left across a bus or cycle lane, check for any vehicles, especially cycles, that may be using it and approaching from behind.

When you approach a roundabout, look out for traffic already on it, especially cyclists or motorcyclists who are less easily seen.

Always *give way* to traffic on your right as this car is doing (unless road markings indicate otherwise), but *keep moving* if the way is clear.

At junctions with more than one roundabout, as above, apply the normal rules for roundabouts at each one, keeping a special look out for 'Give Way' lines.

111

Where there are two lanes at the entrance to a roundabout, unless signs or road markings indicate otherwise:

When turning left:
Approach in the left-hand lane; keep to that lane in the roundabout.

When going forward:
Approach in the left-hand lane; keep to that lane in the roundabout. If conditions dictate (for example, if the left-hand lane is blocked), approach in the right-hand lane; keep to that lane in the roundabout. If the roundabout itself is clear of other traffic, take the most convenient lane through the roundabout.

When turning right:
Approach in the right-hand lane; keep to that lane in the roundabout.

112

When there are more than two lanes at the entrance to a roundabout, unless signs or road markings indicate otherwise, use the clearest convenient lane on approach and through the roundabout suitable for the exit you intend to take.

When turning left at a roundabout with two lanes at the entrance, approach in the left-hand lane and keep to that lane in the roundabout. Do the same when going straight ahead at a roundabout.

Where, for example, the left-hand lane is blocked, approach in the right hand lane and keep to that lane in the roundabout.

When turning right, approach in the right-hand lane and keep to that lane in the roundabout.

At roundabouts with *more* than two lanes at the entrance, choose the most convenient and suitable lane for the exit you intend to take, unless signs or markings tell you to do otherwise.

Procedure at roundabouts with a two-lane entrance. The recommended course in each situation is shown by a solid line: where conditions dictate, drivers may follow the course indicated by the broken line.

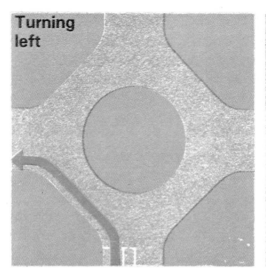

Turning left

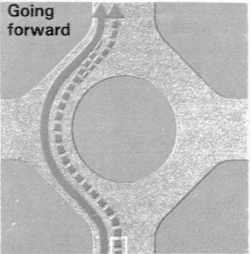

Going forward

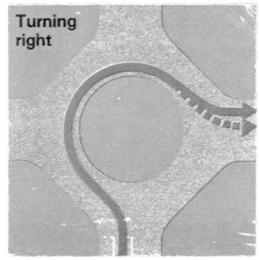

Turning right

113

When in a roundabout, look out for and show consideration to other vehicles crossing in front of you, especially those intending to leave by the next exit. Show particular consideration for cyclists and motorcyclists.

Show consideration to other vehicles crossing in front of you, especially those intending to leave at the next exit.

Particular consideration should be shown for cyclists and motorcyclists.

114

Signals at roundabouts:

When turning left:
Use the left turn indicator on approach and through the roundabout.

When turning left at a roundabout, signal left on the approach to it.

Maintain the signal through the roundabout.

When going forward:
Use the left turn indicator when passing the exit before the one to be taken:

If you are going forward at a roundabout, use the left turn indicator when passing the exit before the one to be taken.

When turning right, indicate right on approach, as above.

When turning right:
Use the right turn indicator on approach, and maintain this signal until passing the exit before the one to be taken. Then change to the left turn indicator.

Maintain this signal until you are passing the exit before the one to be taken.

Then you must change to a left turn indicator.

115

Watch out for cyclists and motorcyclists and give them room. Allow for long vehicles which may have to take a different course, both on the approach to and in the roundabout.

REVERSING

116

Before you reverse, make sure that there are no pedestrians – particularly children – or obstructions in the road behind you. Be especially careful about the 'blind area' behind you – that is, the part of the road which you cannot see from the driving seat.

117

If you cannot see clearly behind, get someone to guide you when you reverse.

At any type of roundabout, watch out for cyclists and motorcyclists and give them room.

Make allowance for long vehicles which may have to take a different course on approach to and in the roundabout.

When you are about to reverse, check that there are no pedestrians or obstructions in the road behind you. You will need to look over your shoulder both ways to check the 'blind area' behind you.

When you cannot see clearly behind, get someone to guide you, as above.

118

Never reverse from a side road into a main road. You must not reverse your vehicle for longer than is necessary.

LAMPS

119

You must:

a make sure that all your lamps are clean, that they work and that your headlamps are properly adjusted – badly adjusted headlamps can dazzle road users and lead to accidents.

b use your sidelamps between sunset and sunrise;

c use headlamps at night on all roads where there is no street lighting, on roads where the street lamps are more than 185 metres (200 yards) apart and on roads where the street lamps are not alight;

d use your headlamps or front fog lamps at any time when visibility is *seriously* reduced, that is, generally, reduced to a distance of less than 100 metres.

It is highly dangerous to reverse into a main road.

Always use headlamps at night on all roads.

Always use your headlamps or front fog lamps when visibility is *seriously* reduced (to a distance of less than 100 metres).

REAR FOG LAMPS

120

You must not use your rear fog lamps unless visibility is *seriously* reduced, that is, generally, reduced to a distance of less than 100 metres. Do not use them simply because it is dark or raining or misty.

121

You should also:

a use headlamps at night on lighted motorways and similar high-speed roads;

b use dipped headlamps at night in built-up areas unless the road is well lit;

c always drive so you can stop well within the distance you can see ahead;

d slow down or stop if you are dazzled by approaching headlamps;

e dip your headlamps when meeting other vehicles or road users and before they dazzle the driver of a vehicle travelling in the same direction in front of you.

Only use your rear fog lamps when visibility is seriously reduced (to a distance of less than 100 metres) as shown above. Mere darkness, rain or mist does not justify their use.

FLASHING HEADLAMPS

122

The flashing of headlamps has only one meaning – like sounding your horn it lets another road user know you are there. Do not flash your headlamps for any other reason.

Only ever flash your headlamps to let others know you are there.

USE OF HORN

123

When your vehicle is moving use your horn when it is necessary as a warning of your presence to other road users – but never use it as a rebuke. You must not use your horn when your vehicle is moving between the hours of 23.30 and 07.00 (11.30 pm and 7 am) in a built-up area. When your vehicle is stopped on the road you may only use your horn at times of danger due to another vehicle moving.

Use your horn only when you need to warn others of your presence. Never use it as a rebuke.

WAITING AND PARKING

124

You MUST NOT let your vehicle stand:

- on a motorway, except on the hard shoulder in an emergency;

- on the carriageway of any pedestrian crossing or within the area marked by zigzag lines on either side of a Zebra or Pelican crossing – except to allow a pedestrian to cross;

- on the carriageway of a 'Clearway' except in an emergency; (see p 128)

- on the right-hand side of the carriageway at night except in a one-way street;

- on the carriageway or the verges of an 'Urban Clearway' during the times shown on the signs (see page 128), other than for no longer than is necessary to let passengers board or alight;

- in a bus lane or cycle lane during its operative times, except to load or unload goods when permitted;

- on the carriageway or the verges of any section of road marked with double white lines even if one of the lines is broken (see page 132) except to let passengers board or alight or to load or unload goods;

- on the side of the carriageway or on the pavement or verge along that side of the road where there are yellow lines near the edge (see

Do *not* let your vehicle stand on a motorway, except on the hard shoulder in an emergency.

Nor should you let it stand on the carriageway of a 'Clearway' such as this, except in an emergency.

Do *not* park in a bus or cycle lane when it is in operation, except to load or unload goods when permitted.

Do *not* park on the carriageway or verges of any section of road marked with double white lines even if one of the lines is broken, except to drop off or pick up passengers or to unload goods.

page 132) during the times shown on the plates on that side of the road, except while passengers board or alight or while loading or unloading goods. In controlled parking zones the standard times

applying throughout the zone are shown on the entry signs (see page 132) and roadside time plates are erected only where different times apply. Also, you must not wait to load or unload goods where there are marks on the kerb (see page 133) during the times shown on the 'No loading' plates; the absence of a yellow line does not automatically mean that parking is permitted there. Certain concessions are allowed to disabled people, whose vehicles can be recognised by the orange badge (see page 134);

- in parking areas in a 'Disc Zone' (indicated on signs) unless it displays a parking disc; the traffic signs at the entry roads to the zone and time plates at the parking places within the zone will indicate the days and times when the scheme is in operation, the time allowed for parking and the period during which return to that parking place is prohibited. These details may vary in different zones;

- in parking places reserved for specific users, for example residents or disabled badge holders – unless you are entitled to use these spaces;

- between 07.00 and 19.00 (7 am and 7 pm) at bus stops marked by a wide yellow line unless it is a bus or coach authorised to stop there;

- on any verge, central reservation or footway, if it is a goods vehicle with a maximum laden weight (including any trailer) exceeding 7.5 tonnes, except in certain circumstances, for example, of loading or unloading could only be performed there and the vehicle is not left unattended.

Never park on the side of a carriageway or on the pavement or verge along the side of a road where there are yellow lines near the edge.

You must *never* park in parking places reserved for specific users (unless you are properly entitled to), for example residents or disabled badge holders.

Do *not* let your vehicle stand in parking areas in a 'Disc Zone' (indicated on signs as above), unless it displays a parking disc.

You must not let your vehicle stand on *any* verge, central reservation or footway. This car is *illegally* parked.

125

Also do not let your vehicle stand:

- where it would cause danger to other vehicles or pedestrians, for example:
  - at or near a school entrance or a school crossing patrol – not even to pick up or set down passengers;
  - where it would hide a traffic sign;
  - on a footpath, pavement or cyclepath;
  - at or near a bus stop;
  - on or near a level crossing;

Never park outside or near a school entrance or school crossing patrol – not even to pick up or drop off passengers.

Do *not* park where your vehicle would hide a traffic sign from the view of other road users.

You must *not* park at or near any bus stop.

● where it would make it difficult for others to see clearly, for example, near or at:

— a junction, ie not within 15 metres of it;
— a bend;
— the brow of a hill;
— a hump-back bridge;

It is extremely dangerous to park on or near a level crossing.

Never park near or at a junction, ie not within 15 metres of it.

By parking on a bend, the driver of this car has created a potentially dangerous situation for traffic going in both directions.

- where it would make the road narrow, for example:
  - opposite a traffic island;
  - alongside another stationary vehicle;
  - opposite or nearly opposite another stationary vehicle if this would narrow the road to less than the width of two vehicles;
  - near roadworks;
- where it would hold up traffic or inconvenience others for example:

  - on a narrow road;
  - on flyovers, in tunnels or in underpasses;
  - on fast main roads, except in a lay-by;
  - on a single-track road, or in a passing place on such a road;
  - blocking a vehicle entrance to properties;
  - blocking the entrance to or exit from a car park;
  - where it would prevent the use of properly parked vehicles;

Do *not* park opposite or nearly opposite another stationary vehicle where this narrows the road to less than the width of two vehicles.

It is inconsiderate and illegal to park alongside another stationary vehicle.

Parking on a narrow road also creates an obstruction.

● where emergency vehicles stop or
go in and out, for example:

— hospital and ambulance
entrances;
— doctors' entrances;
— police and fire stations;
— fire hydrants;
— entrances to coastguard
stations.

Make sure you always park your
vehicle safely and where it will cause
the least inconvenience to others.
Walk a few yards rather than cause
accidents.

Never block a vehicle entrance to a property.

You must *not* park where it would prevent others
from leaving proper parking places.

Do *not* obstruct the path of emergency vehicles by
parking in hospital and ambulance entrances.

Always avoid parking near fire hydrants.

126

If your vehicle is fitted with a hazard warning device (ie a switch to permit all the direction indicators to flash simultaneously), it may only be used when the vehicle is stationary, to indicate that the vehicle is causing a temporary obstruction to traffic flow (for example, because it has broken down or is being loaded or unloaded). The device must not be used while the vehicle is in motion, nor should it be regarded as providing an excuse for stopping when you should not.

Always check that there is no one on the road who could be hit by your vehicle door when you open it.

Only use your hazard lights when your vehicle is stationary and when it is necessary. They should *not* be used for stopping in an place where you are not allowed to stop (unless you have broken down).

127

Always pull off the road on to a parking area if you can.

128

Before opening any door of a vehicle make sure that there is no one on the road, pavement or footpath close enough to be hit by the door. Be particularly careful about cyclists and motorcyclists. Get out on the side nearer the kerb whenever you can and make sure that your passengers (especially children) do so too.

If you need to, pull off the road and stop in a parking area if you can.

It is just as important to ensure that nobody on the pavement or footpath is close enough to be hit by the door you are about to open.

129

If you have to park on the road, stop as close as you can to the edge. Before leaving your vehicle make sure the handbrake is on firmly, and switch off the engine and headlamps. Always lock your vehicle.

130

Never park on the road at night if it can be avoided. Except as described in Rule 131, it is illegal to park at night without lights and it is particularly dangerous to park on the road in fog. Lights should always be left on in these conditions.

131

Cars, goods vehicles not exceeding 1525 kg unladen, invalid carriages and motorcycles may be parked at night without lights on a road subject to a speed limit of 30 mph or less, but only if:

a the vehicle is at least 10 metres away from a junction, close and parallel to the kerb and facing in the direction of traffic flow; or

b it is in a recognised parking place.

Trailers and vehicles with projecting loads must not be left without lights on a road at night.

When you do stop on the road, always try to park as close to the kerb as you can.

If you can avoid doing so, never park on the road at night. It is very difficult for other road users to see your vehicle in the dark.

BREAKDOWNS AND ACCIDENTS

132

If you have a breakdown, think first of other traffic. Get your vehicle off the road if possible and keep your passengers and yourself off the road.

133

Take steps to warn other drivers of an obstruction. If your vehicle is fitted with hazard warning lights, use them. If you carry a red warning sign (a reflecting triangle), place it on the road at least 50 metres (150 metres on the hard shoulder of motorways) before the obstruction, and on the same side of the road. If you carry warning devices such as traffic cones, place them on the road to guide traffic past the obstruction. The first should be about 15 metres from the obstruction and next to the kerb. The last should be level with the outside of the obstruction. At night or in poor visibility, do not stand at the rear of your vehicle or allow anyone else to do so – you may obscure the rear lamps.

When you break down, try and get your vehicle off the road and keep your passengers and yourself off the road. Think of other traffic.

If your vehicle has hazard warning lights, use them, as shown here.

If you carry a red warning sign (a reflecting triangle), place it on the road at least 50 metres back from your vehicle and on the same side of the road. If you carry cones, the first should be placed 15 metres back from your vehicle by the kerb.

On the hard shoulder of motorways, you should place a red warning sign 150 metres back from your vehicle.

134

If anything falls from your vehicle, stop as soon as you can with safety and remove it from the carriageway.

135

There may have been an accident if you see several vehicles in the distance which are going very slowly or have stopped, or if you see warning signs and the flashing lights of emergency vehicles. Slow down and be prepared to stop.

136

If you are first on the scene of an accident you should:

a warn other traffic by displaying a red triangle and/or traffic cones, and by switching on hazard warning lights or other lights, or by any other safe means. Extinguish lighted cigarettes and other fire hazards, and ask drivers to switch off their engines;

b arrange for the police and ambulance authorities to be summoned immediately with full details of the location and casualties; on a motorway, if necessary drive on to the next emergency telephone;

c remove casualties if in any further immediate danger but do not move them unnecessarily; give first aid as described on page 73;

Should anything fall from your vehicle, stop as soon as you safely can and retrieve it.

When you see warning signs and the flashing lights of emergency vehicles, there may have been an accident, so slow down and be prepared to stop.

When first at the scene of an accident, warn other traffic by displaying warning signs and switching on hazard lights, as below.

If you are on a motorway, drive on to the next emergency telephone if necessary, to call the emergency services.

d get uninjured people out of the vehicles and into a place of safety; on a motorway this should be away from the carriageway or

hard shoulder or central reservation;

e stay at the scene until emergency services arrive.

Once you've learned to drive, this is how to stay on the road.

The first time you go out on your own, take Britain's most advanced motoring organisation with you. To join or for details of all our services please telephone us free on 0800 400 432.

THE NEW KNIGHTS OF THE ROAD

Accidents involving dangerous goods

137

If the accident involves a vehicle containing dangerous goods (the vehicle may display a hazard information panel as shown on page 134 and often will have other information such as the name of the substance being carried), you should also:

a arrange for the police or fire brigade to be given immediately as much additional information as possible about the labels and other markings;

b keep everyone well away from the vehicle; even if you act to save life do so with the utmost caution as dangerous liquids may be leaking on to the highway; beware also of dangerous dust or vapours being carried towards you by the wind.

138

Make sure your cycle is safe to ride. Never ride a cycle which is too large or too small for you to control properly. At night you must show front and rear lamps and a rear reflector. Your brakes, lamps and reflector must be kept in proper working order. Make sure your tyres are in good condition and are properly pumped up and that your chain is properly adjusted and lubricated. It is a good idea to fit a bell to your cycle and to use it, if necessary, to warn other people on the road that you are coming.

Make sure that your cycle is in good working order and safe to ride.

Always look round and make sure that it is safe to move away from the kerb before you start to ride.

139

Before starting to ride, always look around and make sure that it is safe to move away from the kerb. Before turning right or left, moving out to pass or pulling up at the kerb, always look behind and make sure it is safe. Give a clear arm signal to show what you intend to do. Look ahead for obstructions in the road such as drains or potholes so that you do not have to swerve suddenly to avoid them.

Before attempting any kind of manoeuvre, always look behind and make sure it is safe.

Give a clear arm signal to show what you intend to do. Because cyclists are less easily seen by other road users, it is of extra importance that you signal clearly.

Extra rules for cyclists

140

Do not ride more than two side by side. Ride in single file on narrow roads. You must not ride on the pavement or on a footpath unless there are signs allowing shared use with pedestrians.

141

On busy roads and at night, if you want to turn right it is often safer to stop first on the left-hand side of the road. Wait for a safe gap in the traffic before you start to turn.

142

You may only use a bus lane where the signs show the symbol of a bicycle. You must not use other bus lanes.

Never ride more than two side by side, as shown here.

If you want to turn right it is sometimes safer to stop on the left-hand side of a busy road and wait for a gap in the traffic.

Cyclists may only use a bus lane where signs show the symbol of a bicycle, as they do here. Otherwise, bus lanes are out of bounds.

143

You may, if you wish, follow the procedure in Rules 110–115 for roundabouts. But if, because of inexperience or for any other reason, you feel unable to do so, you should either stay in the left-hand lane of the roundabout and look out particularly for vehicles crossing your path to leave the roundabout, or get off your cycle and walk.

144

Remember that you cannot be seen as easily as larger vehicles and that you should always give clear arm signals to let drivers behind you know what you intend to do, especially at roundabouts and junctions.

You may either follow the procedure in Rules 110–115 for roundabouts, or, if you feel you cannot because of inexperience or another reason, you can stay in the left-hand lane of the roundabout, until you reach your exit.

Clear arm signals are essential to let drivers behind you know what you intend to do.

145

When you are riding:

a always keep both hands on the handlebar unless you are signalling;

b always keep both feet on the pedals;

c do not hold on to another vehicle or another cyclist;

d do not carry a passenger unless your cycle has been built or altered to carry one;

e do not ride close behind another vehicle;

f do not carry anything which might affect your balance or become entangled with the wheels or chain;

g do not lead an animal;

h wear light-coloured or reflective and fluorescent clothing (see Rule 4).

Keep both hands on the handlebar at all times, unless you are signalling.

Do *not* ride close behind another vehicle, as it could stop suddenly.

It is dangerous to hold on to another vehicle or another cyclist.

146

If there is a suitable cycle path, ride on it.

Avoid carrying anything which affects your balance or may become entangled with the wheels or chain, such as shopping bags.

Always wear light-coloured or reflective and fluorescent clothing while cycling and you will be much more easily seen by other road users.

Cycle paths allow safe and easy riding. If you can use one, do.

The road user in charge of animals

147

Do not let your dog out on its own. When you take it for a walk on the road, keep in on a lead.

148

If you have an animal in your car, keep it under control. Make sure it cannot disturb you while you are driving. Do not let a dog out of a car on to the road unless it is on a lead.

149

Before riding a horse on the roads, make sure you can control it in traffic. When riding, keep to the left. If you are leading a horse, on foot or while riding another, you should also keep to the left and keep the led animal on your left. In one-way streets, proceed only in the direction of the traffic and keep to the left. You must not ride, lead or drive a horse on a footpath or pavement by the side of the road.

Never let your dog out on its own and when you take it for a walk on the road, keep it on a lead.

If you are carrying an animal in your car, keep it under control and make sure it cannot interfere with your driving.

When you are riding a horse on the road, keep well to the left.

If you are leading a horse, while walking or while riding another horse, you should still keep to the left and keep the led animal on your left. You must not ride, lead or drive a horse on a footpath.

Never ride or lead a horse on a footpath or pavement by the side of the road.

150

If you are riding a horse, you should wear a hard hat.

151

If you are riding or herding animals after sunset, you should wear light-coloured or reflective clothing and carry lights which show white to the front and red to the rear.

152

If you are herding animals, keep to the left of the road and if there is someone with you send him along the road to warn drivers at places such as bends and brows of hills where they may not be able to see. If your herd is very large, divide it into smaller groups.

It is essential for protection to wear a hard hat at all times while riding a horse.

If you are herding animals, keep them to the left of the road.

153

Take particular care at level crossings (see Rules 186–198).

At level crossings take particular care and stop when signalled to do so.

*Rules 26-40, 41 (first part), 44,
48-52, 55, 74 (part), 75, 77,
84-86, 90, 119, 120, 121 (part),
122-123, 124 (part), 132-133,
135-137 and 148 also apply to
motorway driving.*

GENERAL

154

Motorways are dual-carriageway roads which must not be used by pedestrians, learner drivers, cyclists and riders of small motorcycles. Slow-moving vehicles, agricultural vehicles and some carriages used by invalids are also prohibited. (See page 143). It is an offence to pick up or set down a passenger or hitch-hiker on any part of a motorway including a slip road.

Remember that certain types of road users are
prohibited from travelling on motorways.

Motorway driving

155

Traffic travels faster on motorways than ordinary roads and you will need to sum up traffic situations more quickly. Using your mirrors and concentrating all the time are doubly important on motorways.

156

Make sure that your vehicle is fit to cruise at speed, and has correct tyre pressures for motorway driving and enough petrol, oil and water to take you at least to the next service area. You must ensure that any loads carried or towed are secure.

157

Slip roads and link roads between motorways may have sharp bends which you can take safely only by reducing speed.

Motorway driving, more than any other, requires your full concentration at all times, as well as the careful and constant use of mirrors.

Do not forget how fast you are travelling as you may encounter a sharp bend in a slip road which you can only take safely by reducing speed.

JOINING THE MOTORWAY

158

When you join the motorway other than at its start, you will normally approach from a road on the left (a slip road). Give way to traffic already on the motorway. Watch for a safe gap in the traffic in the left-hand lane on the motorway and then adjust your speed in the extra lane (the acceleration lane) so that when you join it you are already travelling at the same speed. If there is not a suitable gap, wait in the acceleration lane until it is safe to enter the motorway.

If you do not join the motorway at its start, you will normally approach from a slip road on the left.

You must give way to traffic already on the motorway and look for a safe gap in the left-hand lane to move into when you have reached the correct speed.

159

After joining the motorway, stay in the left-hand lane long enough to get used to the speed of traffic before trying to overtake.

ON THE MOTORWAY

160

You must not reverse or turn in the road, or cross the central reservation, or drive against the traffic.

Never turn around on a motorway.

Never cross the central reservation.

161

Even if you have missed your turn-off point or have taken the wrong route you must carry on until you reach the next exit.

Never attempt to drive against the traffic.

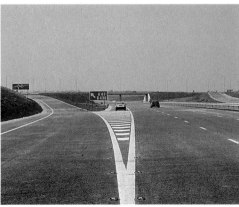

If you miss your exit, do *not* reverse back.

162

IN good visibility and weather conditions, drive at a steady cruising speed within the limits of your vehicle. You must not break the speed limits for the motorways or for your vehicle. On wet or icy roads, or in fog, keep your speed down.

When road and weather conditions are good, drive at a steady cruising speed according to the limits of your vehicle.

Do *not* break the speed limit for the motorways or for your vehicle.

163

Driving for long distances may make you feel sleepy. To help prevent this, make sure there is plenty of fresh air in your vehicle or stop at a service area, or turn off at an exit, and walk around.

When road and weather conditions are bad, keep your speed down.

Should you feel at all sleepy while driving on the motorway, let some fresh air into your vehicle or stop at a service area, or turn off at an exit and walk around.

Lane discipline
164
On a two-lane carriageway, drive in the left-hand lane except when overtaking.

165
On carriageways with three or more lanes the normal 'Keep to the left' rule still applies. You may, however, stay in the middle lane when there are slower vehicles in the left-hand lane, but you should return to the left-hand lane when you have passed them. The right-hand lane is for overtaking only.

If you use it, move back to the middle lane and then into the left-hand lane as soon as you can, but without cutting in.

You may only stay in the middle lane when there are slower vehicles in the left-hand lane, but you should return to the left-hand lane when you have passed them.

Always drive in the left-hand lane except when overtaking.

The right-hand lane is for overtaking *only*. If you use it, move back to the middle lane and then the left-hand lane as soon as you can.

166

To help drivers on motorways, there are amber-coloured studs marking the right-hand edge of the carriageway, red studs marking the left-hand edge and green studs separating the acceleration and deceleration lanes from the through carriageway.

167

On some motorways, direction signs may be placed over the road. Pay special attention to the signs and move into the correct lane in good time.

Pay particular attention to the signs over the motorway and act on them in good time.

168

A goods vehicle which has an operating weight of more than 7.5 tonnes, or any vehicle drawing a trailer, or a bus longer than 12 metres, must not use the right-hand lane of a carriageway with three or more lanes unless there are exceptional circumstances.

Motorway fog
169

When driving in fog, it is vital that you should obey the rules in Rule 55.

Certain types of vehicles are prohibited from using the right-hand lane of a motorway. This is one of them.

Driving in fog requires special rules (see Rule 55). Obey them at all times.

Overtaking
170

Overtake only on the right, unless traffic is moving in queues and the traffic queue on your right is moving more slowly than you are. Never move to a lane on your left to overtake. Never use the hard shoulder for overtaking.

Overtake *only* on the right, unless a traffic queue on your right is moving more slowly than you are.

171

Do not overtake unless you are sure it is safe for yourself and others. Many accidents on motorways are rear-end collisions. So before you start to overtake make sure that the lane you will be joining is clear far enough behind – use your mirrors – and ahead. Remember that traffic may be coming up behind much more quickly than you think. Signal before you move out. Be particularly careful at dusk, in the dark and in fog or mist, when it is more difficult to judge speed and distance.

Remember:

Mirrors – Signal – Manoeuvre.

Never overtake unless you are sure it is safe for yourself and others. This driver of the white car has *not* made sure.

Always check your mirrors to see what is behind well before pulling out.

172

Get back to the left-hand lane or, if this is occupied, the middle lane as soon as you can after overtaking, but do not cut in on the vehicle you have just overtaken.

Signal *before* you pull out.

Finally, manoeuvre, having ensured it is safe to do so.

Breakdowns
173

If you vehicle breaks down, get it off the carriageway and onto the hard shoulder as quickly as possible, and as far to the left as you can. Never forget the danger from passing traffic, switch on your hazard warning lights, and at night leave your side lights on as well. Do not open the doors nearest to the carriageway and do not stand at the rear of the vehicle or between it and the passing traffic. To get help use the emergency telephones on your side of the motorwaay. Never cross the carriageway to use the emergency telephones. The nearest telephone on your side will be indicated by an arrow on a marker post at the back of the hard shoulder. Don't leave your vehicle unattended for a long period. If you cannot move your vehicle off the carriageway take steps to warn others of its presence (see Rule 133). Drivers will need to decide in the particular circumstances whether to keep passengers in the vehicle or not. If passengers do get out they should not congregate behind the vehicle and should not wander about on the hard shoulder. Children should be kept under strict control. Animals should be kept in the vehicle whenever possible. When rejoining the carriageway, build your speed up first on the hard shoulder. Watch for a safe gap in the traffic before rejoining it.

When your vehicle breaks down, get it onto the hard shoulder as quickly as you can. Switch on your hazard lights and do *not* open the doors nearest to the carriageway.

The nearest telephone will be indicated by an arrow on a marker post at the back of the hard shoulder.

Use the emergency telephones on *your* side of the motorway to call for help.

If you are unable to move your vehicle off the carriageway, attempt to warn others of its presence.

As a driver, you will need to decide whether to keep passengers in the vehicle or not, according to the circumstances. If passengers do get out, they should keep off the hard shoulder and children and animals should be kept under strict control.

Obstructions
174

If anything that may cause danger falls from your vehicle or from another vehicle, use the roadside telephone to inform the police. Do not try to retrieve it yourself.

Should anything fall from your vehicle or another vehicle, inform the police, do *not* try to retrieve it yourself.

Motorway signals
175

Special signals are used on motorways. In normal conditions they are blank. In dangerous conditions, amber lights flash and a panel in the middle of the signal shows either a special temporary maximum speed or which lanes are closed. When the danger has been passed the panel of the next signal will show (without flashing lights) the end of restriction signal.

In dangerous conditions special signals are used on motorways. They have flashing amber lights and show either a special temporary maximum speed or which lanes are closed.

When the danger has been passed, the next signal will show (without flashing lights) the end of restriction.

176

On most motorways, the signals are on the central reservation at intervals of not more than two miles and they apply to all lanes. On some very busy motorways, the signals are overhead, one applying to each lane.

Some very busy motorways have signals overhead,
as above – one applying to each lane.

177

Some signals have red lights as well.
If the red lights above your lane flash,
you must not go beyond the signal in
that lane. If red lights flash on a slip
road, you must not enter it.

Red lights flashing mean you must not
continue in that lane beyond the light.

178

Some motorways still have flashing
amber signals at their entrances and
at one- or two-mile intervals. These
warn of danger; for example, an
accident, fog or risk of skidding. When
the signals are flashing, keep your
speed under 30 mph until you are
sure it is safe to go faster.

When the amber signals are flashing, keep
your speed under 30 mph until you are
sure it is safe to go faster.

179

These signals are for your safety. Always act on them. Remember – danger may be present even if you cannot see the cause.

ROADSIDE SIGNALS

Temporary
maximum speed

Lane closed
ahead

End of restriction

OVERHEAD SIGNALS

1

2

3

4

5

1 Temporary maximum speed
2 Change lane
3 Leave motorway at next exit
4 Do not proceed any further
  in this lane
5 End of restriction

Stopping and parking
180
You MUST NOT stop except:

a in an emergency (for example, to prevent an accident);

b when you break down (see Rules 132 and 173);

c when you are signalled to do so by the police, by an emergency traffic sign or by flashing red light signals.

Never stop on motorways except in an emergency. In this case, to avoid an accident ahead.

Stopping when you break down obviously cannot be avoided.

When you are signalled to do so by police, you must stop.

181

You may park only at a service area. You must not park on:

a the carriageway itself;

b the slip roads;

c the hard shoulders (except in an emergency);

d the central reservation.

The only place you may park legally on a motorway is at a service area.

Never park on the carriageway itself.

Nor on slip roads.

182

You must not walk on the carriagewaay. In an emergency be particularly careful to keep children and animals off the carriageway and the hard shoulders.

ROADWORKS

183

Special care is needed at roadworks. Observe signs, signals and speed limits. Check your mirrors, get into lane early and adjust your speed appropriately. Keep a safe distance from the vehicle in front (see Rule 51).

When approaching roadworks, observe and act on all signs, signals and speed limits in good time.

Do *not* walk on the carriageway.

Adjust your speed and keep a safe distance from the vehicle in front.

LEAVING THE MOTORWAY

184

If you are not going to the end of the motorway you will normally leave by a slip road on your left. Watch for the signs letting you know you are getting near your turn-off point. If you are not already in the left-hand lane, move into it well before reaching your turn-off point and stay in it. Give a left turn signal in good time and, if necessary, reduce speed. Then get into the extra lane provided (the deceleration lane) where you can slow down before you join the slip road.

When leaving the motorway, get into the left-hand lane well in advance of reaching your turn-off point.

Give a left turn signal in good time.

185

When leaving the motorway or using a link road remember to adjust your driving to suit the new conditions. Your speed will be higher than you think – 50 mph may feel like 30 mph – so be sure to use your speedometer.

When nearing your exit, get into the extra lane provided, where you can slow down before you join the slip road.

On leaving the motorway, adjust your driving to suit the new conditions. Watch your speed in particular as you will be travelling faster than you think.

The road user and railway level crossings

GENERAL

186

Approach a level crossing at a moderate speed and cross it with care. Do not loiter. Never drive 'nose to tail' over it. Never drive on to one unless you can see the road is clear on the other side. Never stop on or immediately beyond any level crossing.

Always approach a level crossing at a moderate speed and cross it with care.

Never drive 'nose to tail' over the crossing.

187

Most modern level crossings have steady amber and twin flashing red traffic lights. *Always* obey these traffic lights and stop at the white line if the red lights are flashing. Invariably a train will be coming, and if there are barriers, they will be lowered.

You must not stop on or immediately beyond any level crossing.

At any type of level crossing, you must *always* obey the traffic light signals and stop at the white line or barriers if there are any.

AUTOMATIC HALF-BARRIER LEVEL CROSSINGS

188

These crossings have automatic barriers across the left side of the road. These are operated by the train and lower automatically just before the train reaches the crossing. Amber lights and an audible alarm followed by flashing red 'STOP' lights warn you when the barriers are about to come down. Do not move on to the railway once these signals have started – the train cannot stop and will be at the crossing very soon. Wait at the 'STOP' line. If you are on foot, wait at the barrier, or the broken white line on the road or footpath. Never zig-zag around the barriers – you could be killed and endanger other lives. If one train has gone by, but the barriers stay down, the red lights continue to flash and the audible alarm changes in tone, you must wait as another train will soon arrive.

189

If you are already crossing when the amber lights and alarm start, keep going.

Automatic half-barrier crossings look like this. Amber lights and an audible alarm followed by flashing red lights warn you when the barriers are about to come down.

Wait at the 'STOP' line and continue to wait if the barriers stay down and the lights continue flashing. This means that another train is approaching.

If you are already crossing when the alarm sounds and the lights start to flash, keep going.

190

If you are driving a large or slow-moving vehicle, or if you are herding animals, first telephone the signalman, to get his permission to cross. There is a special railway telephone at the crossing. If you have telephoned the signalman before crossing, telephone him again to tell him when you are clear of the railway.

191

If the barriers stay down at any time for more than three minutes without a train arriving, use the telephone at the crossing to ask the signalman's advice.

192

If your vehicle stalls, or breaks down, or if you have an accident on the crossing:

First: Get everyone out of the vehicle and clear of the crossing; then use the telephone at the crossing immediately to tell the signalman.

Second: If there is time, move the vehicle clear of the crossing. Contact the signalman again to let him know when the crossing is clear. If the alarm sounds, or the amber light shows, get everyone well clear of the crossing.

If, for some reason, you are stranded on the crossing, get everyone out of the vehicle and clear of the crossing. Inform the signalman and if there is time, move the vehicle off the crossing.

You must get the permission of the signalman to cross if you are driving a large or slow-moving vehicle. Once you have crossed, you must inform him that you are clear of the railway.

Use the telephone at the crossing to ask the signalman's advice should the barrier stay down without a train arriving.

AUTOMATIC OPEN CROSSINGS

193

Some level crossings without gates, barriers or attendant have amber lights and an audible alarm followed by flashing red 'STOP' lights. When the alarm sounds and the lights show you must stop and wait. Do not cross the railway – a train will reach the crossing shortly. If one train has gone by, but the lights continue to flash, you must wait as another train will soon arrive. The lights will go out when it is safe to cross. At some crossings there is a special sign before the crossing and a special railway telephone at the crossing. At these crossings if you are driving a very large or slow vehicle, or are herding animals, you must first telephone the signalman to make sure it is safe for you to cross. Contact him again to tell him when you are clear of the crossing.

LEVEL CROSSINGS WITH GATES OR FULL BARRIERS

194

Many level crossings have gates, or barriers with skirts, that are operated either by an attendant or by remote control and go right across the road. Some also have amber lights and an audible alarm followed by flashing red 'STOP' lights. Do not pass the lights once they show. If there are no lights at all, stop when the gates begin to close or the barriers start to descend.

Some level crossings are without gates, barriers or attendant, but they have amber lights and an audible alarm followed by flashing red lights.

When the lights continue to flash after a train has gone by, you must wait as another train will soon arrive.

Some crossings with barriers also have amber lights and an audible alarm followed by flashing red lights. Do not cross once the lights have shown.

195

Some level crossings with gates or barriers but no attendant have 'STOP' signs and small red and green lights. Do not cross when the red light is showing, as a train is coming. If the green light is showing, open both gates or fully raise both barriers, and check that the green light is still showing before you cross. Close the gates, or lower the barriers when you have crossed. Where there is a special railway telephone at the crossing and you are driving a very large or slow-moving vehicle, or are herding animals, first telephone the signalman to make sure it is safe for you to cross. When you have crossed, telephone the signalman again to let him know you are over.

Do *not* cross when the red light is showing. When the green light shows, open both gates or raise both barriers, and check that the green light is still showing before you cross.

196

Some level crossings have gates, but no attendant or red lights. At such crossings, stop, look both ways, listen and make sure there is no train coming. If there is a special railway telephone, first telephone the signalman to make sure it is safe for you to cross. If you have telephoned or not, before crossing with a vehicle or animals, open *both* gates wide and then make a further check that no train is coming. Drive your vehicle or animals clear of the crossing and then close both gates. If you have telephoned the signalman, contact him again when you are clear of the railway.

This crossing has gates, but no attendant or red lights. Ensure there is no train coming before you cross.

OPEN LEVEL CROSSINGS

197

At level crossings with no gates, barriers, attendant or traffic lights, there will be a 'Give Way' sign. You must look both ways, listen and make sure ther is no train coming before you cross. Always 'Give Way' to trains.

At this sort of crossing, always look both ways, listen and make sure there is no train coming before you cross.

HORSE RIDERS

198

If you are approaching an automatic crossing and the audible warning sounds, stop well back from the railway. Do not dismount. If you are on the crossing when the warning starts keep going. There is plenty of time to get clear.

If you are on horseback, stop well back from a crossing if it signals for you to do so and wait for the train to pass.

Speed limits

Type of Vehicle	Built-up Areas* M.P.H.	Single carriage-ways M.P.H.	Dual carriage-ways M.P.H.	Motorways M.P.H.
Cars (including car derived vans and motorcycles)	30	60	70	70
Cars towing Caravans or Trailers (including car derived vans and motorcycles)	30	50	60	60
Buses and Coaches (not exceeding 12 metres in overall length)	30	50	60	70
Goods Vehicles (not exceeding 7·5 tonnes maximum laden weight)	30	50	60	70 (60 if articulated or towing a trailer)
Heavy Goods Vehicles (exceeding 7·5 tonnes maximum laden weight)	30	40	50	60

These are the national speed limits and apply to all roads unless signs show otherwise.
*The 30 mph limit applies to all traffic on all roads with street lighting unless signs show otherwise.

Light signals controlling traffic
TRAFFIC LIGHT SIGNALS

RED means "Stop". Wait behind the stop line on the carriageway.

RED AND AMBER also means "Stop". Do not pass through or start until GREEN shows.

GREEN means you may go on if the way is clear. Take special care if you mean to turn left or right and give way to pedestrians who are crossing.

AMBER means "Stop" at the stop line. You may go on only if the AMBER appears after you have crossed the stop line or are so close to it that to pull up might cause an accident.

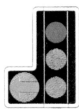

A GREEN ARROW may be provided in addition to the full green signal if movement in a certain direction is allowed before or after the full green phase. If the way is clear you may go but only in the direction shown by the arrow. You may do this whatever other lights may be showing.

FLASHING RED LIGHTS

Alternately flashing red lights mean YOU MUST STOP

At level crossings, lifting bridges, airfields, fire stations, etc.

Signals by authorised persons
Come on

Beckoning on a vehicle from the front

Beckoning on a vehicle from the side

Beckoning on a vehicle from behind

Stop

Vehicle approaching from the front

Vehicles approaching from both front and behind

Vehicle approaching from behind

Signals to other road users

DIRECTION INDICATOR SIGNALS

 I intend to move out to the right or turn right

 I intend to move in to the left or turn left or stop on the left

STOP LIGHT SIGNALS

 I am slowing down or stopping

ARM SIGNALS

For use when direction indicator signals are not used; or when necessary to reinforce direction indicator signals and stop lights. Also for use by pedal cyclists and those in charge of horses.

 I intend to move out to the right or turn right

 I intend to move in to the left or turn left

 I intend to slow down or stop This signal is particularly important at Zebra crossings to let other road users, including pedestrians, know that you are slowing down or stopping.

ARM SIGNALS TO PERSONS CONTROLLING TRAFFIC

 I want to go straight on

I want to turn left

 I want to turn right

Traffic signs SIGNS GIVING ORDERS

These signs are mostly circular and those with red circles are mostly prohibitive

Signs with blue circles but no red border mostly give positive instruction

Maximum speed

National speed limit applies

Stop and Give Way

Give way to traffic on major road

School crossing patrol

No vehicles

No entry for vehicular traffic

No right turn

No left turn

No U turns

Vehicles may pass either side to reach same destination

Route to be used by pedal cycles only

Keep left (right if symbol reversed)

No overtaking

Give priority to vehicles from opposite direction

No motor vehicles

No motor vehicles except solo motorcycles, scooters or mopeds

Manually operated temporary 'STOP' sign

No vehicles with over 12 seats except regular scheduled, school and works buses

Share pedal cycle and pedestrian route

With-flow pedal cycle lane

One-way traffic (Note: compare circular "Ahead" sign)

No cycling

No pedestrians

No goods vehicles over maximum gross weight shown (in tonnes)

No vehicles including load over weight shown (in tonnes)

Axle weight limit in tonnes

No vehicles over height shown

Ahead only

Turn left (right if symbol reversed)

Turn left ahead (right if symbol reversed)

No vehicle or combination of vehicles over length shown

No vehicles over width shown

No stopping (Clearway)

Parking restricted to use by people named on sign

No stopping during times shown except for as long as necessary to set down or pick up passengers

Minimum speed

End of minimum speed

Mini-roundabout (roundabout circulation – give way to vehicles from the immediate right)

End of restriction

Exception for loading/unloading goods

Exception for vehicles with over 12 seats

Exception for stage and scheduled express carriages, school and works buses

Exception for access to premises and land adjacent to the road where there is no alternative route

With-flow bus and cycle lane

Contra-flow bus lane

WARNING SIGNS *Mostly triangular*

Cross roads

Roundabout

T junction

Staggered junction

Cycle route ahead

Slippery road

Change to opposite carriageway (may be reversed)

Accompanied horses or ponies crossing the road ahead

Double bend first to left (may be reversed)

Level crossing without barrier or gate ahead

Road works

Hump bridge

Cattle

Wild animals

Traffic merges from left/right

Road narrows on both sides

Two-way traffic crosses one-way road

Two-way traffic straight ahead

Quayside or river bank

Opening or swing bridge ahead

Falling or fallen rocks

Height limit (e.g. low bridge)

Available width of headroom indicated

Low-flying aircraft or sudden aircraft noise

Dual carriageway ends

Road narrows on right (left if symbol reversed)

Humps for ½ mile

Distance over which road humps extend

Pedestrian crossing

Ford
Worded warning sign

Loose chippings

Wild horses or ponies

Failure of light signals

Traffic signals

REDUCE SPEED NOW
Plate below some signs

Sharp deviation of route to left (or right if chevrons reversed)

Bend to right (or left if symbol reversed)

1 mile

Distance to tunnel

Level crossing with barrier or gate ahead

AUTOMATIC BARRIERS STOP when lights show
Plate to indicate a level crossing equipped with automatic barriers and flashing lights

Level crossing without barrier (the additional lower half of the cross is used when there is more than one railway line)

Steep hill downwards

Steep hill upwards

Gradients may be shown as a ratio i.e. 20% = 1:5

School
Children going to or from school

Uneven road

Risk of Grounding
Risk of grounding of long low vehicles at level crossing

Safe height 16'-6"
Overhead electric cable; plate indicates maximum height of vehicles which can pass safely

Elderly people
Crossing point for elderly people (blind or disabled if shown)

No footway for 400 yds
Pedestrians in road ahead

Fallen tree
Other danger; plate indicates nature of danger

Patrol
School crossing patrol ahead (Some signs have amber lights which flash when patrol is operating)

STOP 100 yds
Distance to "STOP" line ahead

GIVE WAY 50 yds
Distance to "Give Way" line ahead

DIRECTION SIGNS
Signs on motorways

End of motorway

At a junction leading directly
into a motorway

Mostly rectangular
Blue backgrounds

M1
The North
Sheffield 32
Leeds   59

Route confirmatory sign
after junction

M23

Start of motorway and point
from which motorway
regulations apply

The North
Sheffield
Leeds

Nottingham
A52

25

On approaches to junctions
(junction number on black
background)

A404 Marlow   Oxford   M40

Downwards pointing arrow means
"Get in lane"

A46 (M69) Coventry (E) & Leicester

The NORTH WEST. Coventry (N) & B'ham   M6

The panel with the slopping arrow
indicates the destinations which can
be reached by leaving the motorway
at the next junction

Signs on primary routes
Green backgrounds

On approaches to junctions
(The blue panel indicates that
the motorway commences from
the junction ahead. The motorway
shown in brackets can also
be reached by proceeding
in that direction)

 Zoo

Tourist attraction

 300 yds

Picnic site

A46
Lincoln   12
Newark   28
(Nottingham 48)
Leicester   63

Route confirmatory sign
after junction

Other direction signs

300 yds

Direction to camping
and caravan site

 Wrest Park

Ancient monument in the
care of English Heritage

 ◼ ▲ ◆ ●

Emergency diversion
route for motorway
traffic

(A33,M3)

Advisory route for lorries

Signs on non-primary routes
Black borders

Hemel
Hempstead 7
B 486

At the junction

 R

Ring road

Matlock A625
Bradwell (A622)

Bradwell
B6049

On approach to junctions
(a symbol may sometimes be
shown to indicate a warning
of a hazard or prohibition on a
road leading from a junction)

Sutton C'field
A38
Tamworth
(A 4091)

At the junction

 R   A46

Ring road   Route
confirmatory
sign
after junction

↑ Scarborough
   A64
← Pickering
   A169
York A64 →

On approaches to junctions

 Council Offices
Public Library

Route for pedestrians

 Marton   3

Recommended route for pedal
cycles to place shown

 Northtown

Diversion route

HR

Holiday route

Local direction signs
Blue borders

↑ Northchurch 1½
  Wigginton   4
← Chesham 5
Potten End 2
Gaddesden 3½
Ashridge   4

On approaches to junctions

 Gatwick 2

Airport

Ring road
Victoria Stn
Cringleford 2½

At the junction

 Toilets

Direction to toilets
with access for the disabled

INFORMATION SIGNS *All rectangular*

"Count-down" markers at exit from motorway
(each bar represents 100 yards to the exit).
Green backed markers may be used on primary
routes and white backed markers with red bars
on the approaches to concealed level crossings

Recommended route
for pedal cycles

Tourist
information
point

Appropriate traffic lanes
at junction ahead

No through
road

Hospital
ahead

Permanent
reduction in
available lanes,
e.g. two-lane
carriageway
reducing to one

Temporary lane closure

Bus lane on road
at junction ahead

Priority over vehicles
from opposite
direction

Advance warning of
restriction or prohibition
ahead

Motorway Service Area Sign
Incorporating the operator's name
(The current price of petrol may be
shown or may be omitted)

The number and position of arrows and red
bars may be varied according to lanes open
and closed

Lane control signals

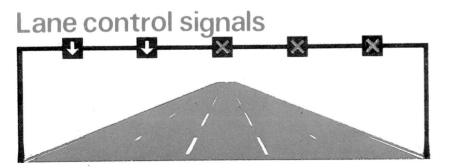

White arrows – lane available to traffic facing the sign. Red crosses – lane closed to traffic facing sign.

Entrance to
controlled
parking zone

End of
controlled
parking zone

One-way street

Parking place for
towed caravans

Road markings
ACROSS THE CARRIAGEWAY

Give way to traffic on major road

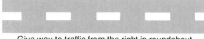

Give way to traffic from the right in roundabout

Give way to traffic from right at mini-roundabout

Stop line at "STOP" sign

Stop line at signals or police control

ALONG THE CARRIAGEWAY

Double white lines   Diagonal stripes   Lane markings

See rules 71 and 72   See rule 73   Lane line See Rules 74 and 75   Centre line   Hazard warning line See Rule 70

ALONG THE EDGE OF THE CARRIAGEWAY

Waiting restrictions

No waiting on carriageway, pavement or verge (except to load or unload or while passengers board or alight) at times shown on nearby plates or on entry signs to controlled parking zones.
If no days are indicated on the sign, the restrictions are in force every day including Sundays and Bank Holidays. The lines give a guide to the restriction in force but the time plates must be consulted.

No waiting for at least eight hours between 7 am and 7 pm on four or more days of the week

No waiting for at least eight hours between 7 am and 7 pm on four or more days of the week plus some additional period outside these times

During any other periods

Examples of plates indicating restriction times

At any time

Continuous prohibition

Mon-Sat 8 am-6·30 pm

Plate giving times

Mon - Sat 8 am - 6 pm Waiting limited to 20 minutes Return prohibited within 40 minutes

Limited waiting

ON THE KERB AT THE EDGE OF THE CARRIAGEWAY

Loading restrictions

No loading or unloading at times shown on nearby plates. If no days are indicated on the sign, the restrictions are in force every day including Sundays and Bank Holidays.

During every working day

During every working day, and additional times

During any other periods

For example

No loading
Mon-Sat
8·30 am-6·30 pm

For example

No loading
at any time

For example

No loading
Mon-Fri
8 00-9 30 am
4 30-6 30 pm

ZEBRA CONTROLLED AREAS

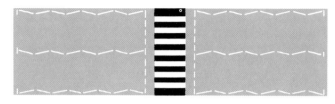

OTHER ROAD MARKINGS

Keep entrance clear of stationary vehicles, even if picking up or setting down children

Indication of traffic lanes

Box junction
See Rule 99

KEEP CLEAR

Do not block entrance
to side road

Parking space reserved
for vehicles named

Warning of "Give Way"
just ahead

See Rule 124

See Rule 82

Vehicle markings
ORANGE BADGE SCHEME

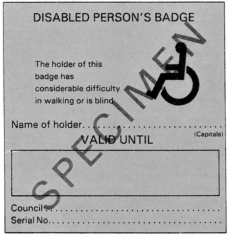

DISABLED PERSON'S BADGE

The holder of this badge has considerable difficulty in walking or is blind

Name of holder........................... (Capitals)

VALID UNTIL

Council.........................
Serial No.........................

SPECIMEN

Windscreen badge for disabled persons entitled to parking concessions (see Rule 124)

PROJECTION MARKERS

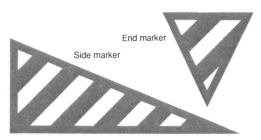

End marker

Side marker

Both required when load or equipment (e.g. crane jib) overhangs front or rear by more than 2 metres

TRANSPORT HAZARD INFORMATION SYSTEM

Certain vehicles carrying dangerous goods must display hazard information panels

2YE
1089
Newtown-on-Moors
(0123) 45678

FLAMMABLE LIQUID

The panel illustrated is for a flammable liquid. Diamond symbols indicating other risks include:

Oxidizing substance   Toxic substance

Radioactive substance   Corrosive substance

Spontaneously combustible substance   Non-flammable compressed gas

IF A SPILLAGE OCCURS –
KEEP WELL AWAY AND INFORM THE POLICE OR FIRE BRIGADE

HEAVY GOODS VEHICLE REAR-MARKINGS

Motor-vehicles over 7500 kilograms maximum gross weight and trailers over 3500 kilograms maximum gross weight

Left   Right

The vertical markings are also required to be fitted to builders' skips placed in the road. Commercial vehicle or combination longer than 13 metres (optional on combinations between 11 and 13 metres)

LONG VEHICLE

Left

LONG VEHICLE

Right

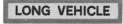

LONG VEHICLE

or

Shortest stopping distances

At 30 mph

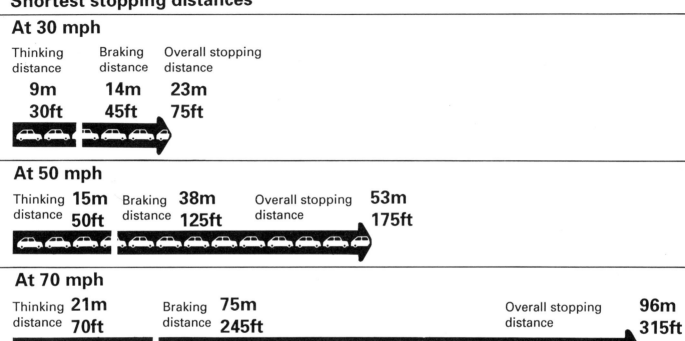

Thinking distance   Braking distance   Overall stopping distance

9m   **14m**   **23m**
30ft   **45ft**   **75ft**

At 50 mph

Thinking **15m**   Braking **38m**   Overall stopping **53m**
distance **50ft**   distance **125ft**   distance **175ft**

At 70 mph

Thinking **21m**   Braking **75m**   Overall stopping **96m**
distance **70ft**   distance **245ft**   distance **315ft**

The distances shown in car lengths are based on an average family saloon.

See also the table following Rule 51 on page 41.

The law's demands

The following pages deal with major points of the law affecting safety on the roads. For the precise wording of the law please refer to the various Acts and Regulations. These are indicated in the margin by the following abbreviations.

CG(S)A	Civic Government (Scotland) Act 1982.
CTA	Cycle Tracks Act 1984.
CUR	Road Vehicles (Construction and Use) Regulations 1986.
DS(RTTC)R	Dangerous Substances (Conveyance by Road in Road Tankers and Tank Containers) Regulations 1981.
GV(PT)R	Goods Vehicles (Plating and Testing) Regulations 1982.
HA	Highway Act 1835, or, as the case may be, Highways Act 1980.
HCVA	Heavy Commercial Vehicles (Controls and Regulations) Act 1973.
HGV(DL)R	Heavy Goods Vehicles (Drivers' Licences) Regulations 1977.
LA	Licensing Act 1872.
MC(PH)R	Motorcyles (Protective Helmets) Regulations 1980.
MT(E&W)R	Motorways (England & Wales) Regulations 1982.
MT(E&W)(A)R	Motorways Traffic (England and Wales) (amendment) Regulations 1984.
MT(SL)R	Motorways Traffic (Speed Limit) Regulations 1974.
MT(S)R	Motorways Traffic (Scotland) Regulations 1964.
MV(T)R	Motor Vehicles (Tests) Regulations 1981.
MV(DL)R	Motor Vehicles (Driving Licences) Regulations 1981
MV(WSB)R	Motor Vehicles (Wearing of Seat Belts) Regulations 1982.
MV(WSBC)R	Motor Vehicles (Wearing of Seat Belts by Children) Regulations 1982.
MV(WSBCRS)R	Motor Vehicles (Wearing of Seat Belts by Children in Rear Seats) Regulations 1989.
PCUR	Pedal Cycles (Construction and Use) Regulations 1983.
PPCRGD	'Pelican' Pedestrian Crossings Regulations and General Directions 1987.
PPVA	Public Passenger Vehicles Act 1981.
R(S)A	Roads (Scotland) Act 1984.
RTA	Road Traffic Act 1988.
RTPDA	Road Traffic (Production of Documents) Act 1985.
RTRA	Road Traffic Regulation Act 1984.
RVLR	Road Vehicles Lighting Regulations 1989.
RV(R and L)R	The Road Vehicles (Registration and Licensing) Regulations 1971.
TSRGD	Traffic Signs Regulations and General Directions 1981.
TA	Transport Acts 1981 and 1982.
VEA	Vehicles (Excise) Act 1971.
ZPCR	'Zebra' Pedestrian Crossings Regulations 1971.

Additional abbreviations: **(E & W)** (England and Wales), **(S)** (Scotland).

TO PEDESTRIANS

You have precedence when you are on the carriageway within the limits of an uncontrolled Zebra crossing, and on a Pelican crossing when the signal to cross is illuminated.
NOTES: (a) An uncontrolled Zebra crossing is one at which traffic is not being controlled by a police constable* and which is marked with two or more lighted beacons, black and white stripes, and studs to indicate the limits of the crossing.
(b) You have NO precedence when you are standing on the kerb or when you are standing on a street refuge or central reservation which is on a Zebra crossing, or on a Pelican crossing when the RED MAN symbol is illuminated.

You *must not*

— loiter on any type of pedestrian crossing;

— wilfully obstruct the free passage along a highway (E & W);

— wilfully obstruct the lawful passage of a person on foot in a public place (S);

— walk on motorways or their slip roads;

— proceed along or across the carriageway when given a direction to stop by a police constable* engaged in controlling traffic;

— without lawful authority or reasonable cause, hold on to or get on a motor vehicle or trailer in motion or tamper with the brake or other part of the mechanism of a motor vehicle;

— be drunk in any highway or public place.

Acts & Regulations
PPCRGD No 9
ZPCR No 8
PPCRGD No 18
ZPCR No 9
HA 1980 Sect 137
CG(S)A Sect 53
MT(E&W)R No 13
MT(S)R No 11
RTA 1988 Sect 37
RTA 1988 Sects 25 and 26
LA Sect 12
CG(S)A Sect 50

TO DOG OWNERS

You *must not*

— allow your dog to be off its lead on a road which has been designated as one where dogs must be kept on a lead, unless your dog is kept for tending sheep or cattle or is in use under proper control for sporting purposes;

— allow your dog to foul a grass verge, a footpath or footway (S).

RTA 1988 Sect 27
CG((S)A Sect 48(1) (a) and (b)

TO HORSE RIDERS

You *must not*

— wilfully ride, lead or drive your horse on a footpath by the side of any road made or set apart for the use of foot passengers (E & W);

— wilfully ride, lead or drive your horse on a footway, footpath or cycle track unless there is a right to do so (S).

HA 1835 Sect 72
R(S)A Sect 129(5)

TO PEDAL CYCLISTS

Before cycling *make sure that*

— your cycle has efficient brakes.

You *must*, even if you are wheeling your cycle

— observe amber† and red 'STOP' signals, traffic signs which give orders, double white lines (solid or broken), yellow road markings and the directions of a police constable* controlling traffic;

PCUR Nos 7–10
RTA 1988 Sect 36 **TSRGD 1981** Nos 7, 23(1) and 34(1) **PPCRGD** No 16 **RTRA** Sects 1, 6, 9 and 53

* The reference to a police constable includes a traffic warden (Transport Act 1968).
† See the illustrations on page 126.

— stop when signalled to do so by a School Crossing Patrol exhibiting a 'STOP – CHILDREN' sign; **RTRA** Sect 28

— give precedence to pedestrians on an uncontrolled Zebra crossing, that is, a crossing marked by black and white stripes, studs and lighted beacons and at which there is no police constable* controlling the traffic; **ZPCR** No 8

— give precedence to pedestrians on a Pelican crossing, when an amber light is flashing. **PPCRGD** No 17

You *must*

— at night, see that your front and rear lamps are lit and that your cycle has an efficient red rear reflector; **RVLR** Nos 18, 23 and 24

— at night, if you are wheeling your cycle or are stationary without lights, keep as close as possible to the nearside edge of the road; **RVLR** No 24

— stop when required to do so by a police constable* in uniform. **RTA 1988** Sect 163

You *must not*

— stop your cycle within the limits of a pedestrian crossing, except in circumstances beyond your control or when it is necessary to do so to avoid an accident; **PPCRGD** No 18 **ZPCR** No 9

— on the approach to an uncontrolled Zebra crossing or Pelican crossing marked by a pattern of zigzag lines, overtake the moving vehicle nearest to the crossing or the leading vehicle which has stopped to give way to a pedestrian on the crossing; **ZPCR** No 10 **PPCRGD** 19

— ride recklessly; **RTA 1988** Sect 28

— ride without due care and attention or without reasonable consideration for other persons using the road; **RTA 1988** Sect 29

— ride under the influence of drink or a drug; **RTA 1988** Sect 30

— wilfully ride on a footpath by the side of any road made or set apart for the use of foot passengers (E & W); **HA 1835** Sect 72

— ride on a footway or footpath unless there is a right to do so (S); **R(S)A** Sect 129(5)

— by negligence or misbehaviour interrupt the free passage of any road user or vehicle; **HA 1835** Sect 78

— leave your cycle on any road in such a way that it is likely to cause danger to other road users; **RTA 1988** Sect 22

— leave your cycle where waiting is prohibited; **RTRA** Sects 1, 6 and 9

— carry a passenger on a bicycle not constructed or adapted to carry more than one person; **RTA 1988** Sect 24

— hold on to a motor vehicle or trailer in motion on any road. **RTA 1988** Sect 26

TO DRIVERS OF MOTOR VEHICLES

Before driving, *make sure that*

— your vehicle is properly licensed and the tax disc displayed (this is necessary even if it is only parked on a public road); **VEA** Sects 1 and 12(4)

— your use of the vehicle is properly insured and that there are no restrictions in the relevant insurance policy (for example, as to who may drive it) which would make your use of the vehicle illegal; **RTA 1988** Sect 143

— You have a current driving licence valid for the type of vehicle you wish to drive. A provisional licence will not show entitlement to ride a motorcycle unless you request it. **RTA 1988** Sects 87 and 110 **PPVA** Sect 22 **TA 1981** Sect 23

* The reference to a police constable includes a traffic warden (Transport Act 1968).

— you have signed your driving licence in ink.

MV(DL)R No 11
and
HGV(DL)R No 7

— you have a current test certificate for your vehicle if it is over the prescribed age limit, and, where applicable, you have a current plating certificate for your goods vehicle;

RTA 1988 Sects 45, 47, 49 and 53
MV(T)R
GV(PT)R

— your eyesight is up to the standard required for the driving test;

RTA 1988 Sect 96
MV(DL)R 1981 No 22(1) (f)

— you have reported to the licensing authority, any health condition likely to affect your driving;

RTA 1988 Sect 94

— the condition of your vehicle, of any trailer it is drawing and of any load, and the number of passengers and the way in which they are carried, are such that they do not endanger yourself or others;

CUR No 100

— your brakes and steering are in good working order and properly adjusted;

CUR No 18

— your tyres are suitable for the vehicle, are properly inflated, have a continuous tread depth of at least 1 mm across three quarters of the width, with visible tread across the remainder of the width, and are free from cuts and other defects;

CUR No 27

— your windscreens and other windows comply with regulations concerning visual transmission of light and freedom from obstruction to vision; and are kept clean, where appropriate, in conjunction with windscreen wipers and washers which should be maintained in effective working order at all times;

CUR Nos 30, 31, 32 and 34

— your seat belts, anchorages, fastenings and adjusting devices are maintained free from obvious defects;

CUR No 48

— your vehicle is fitted with the appropriate number of mirrors, so fitted that you can see traffic behind you;

CUR No 33

— your horn is in working order;

CUR No 37

— your speedometer is in working order;

CUR No 36

— your exhaust system is efficient;

CUR No 54

— any audible anti-theft device that may be fitted complies with the regulations;

CUR No 37(8)

— the load on your vehicle is so secured that neither danger nor nuisance is caused by its falling or being blown off, or shifting;

CUR No 100

— your load if it projects sideways or to the front or rear is not of illegal width or length and at night any extra front and rear lamps are carried and are lit;

CUR Nos 81 and 82
RVLR Nos 21, 22, 23 and 24

— the overall travelling height is recorded in the cab (certain kinds of vehicles only);

CUR No 10

— your vehicle has lamps and reflectors which comply with the regulations and are in working order;

RVLR Nos 18 and 23

— your headlamps are properly adjusted;

RVLR No 23

— your vehicle, if a private car or other vehicle to which the regulation applies, is fitted with seat belts, which must be maintained in good condition;

CUR No 47

— your vehicle, if a road tanker or a vehicle conveying a tank container, carrying a prescribed hazardous substance, displays the required hazard warning panels and that these are kept clean and free from obstruction.

DS(RTTC)R 1981 No 19

When driving *you must*

— wear an approved type of seat belt in any vehicle to which the law applies unless you are exempt from so doing;

RTA 1988 Sect 14
MV(WSB)R 1982
MV(WSBC)R 1982
CUR No 104

— be in such a position that you can exercise proper control over your vehicle and retain a full view of the road and traffic ahead;

— give precedence to a pedestrian who is on an uncontrolled Zebra crossing, that is, a crossing marked by black and white stripes, studs and lighted beacons and at which there is no police constable* controlling the traffic;

ZPCR No 8

— give precedence to pedestrians on a Pelican crossing, when an amber light is flashing;

PPCRGD No 17

— observe speed limits (70 mph on motorways and dual carriageways and 60 mph on all other roads unless a lower limit is indicated by signs or street lighting) or any special speed limit for your vehicle;

RTRA Sects 81, 84, 86, 88, 89 and Sch 6
TA 1982 Sect 61

— observe amber† and red 'STOP' signals, traffic signs which give orders, double white lines, yellow road markings and the directions of a police constable* controlling traffic or giving directions for the purposes of a traffic survey;

TSRGD 1981 Nos 7, 23(1) and 34(1)
PPCRGD No 16
RTRA Sects 1, 6, 9 and 53
RTA 1988 Sects 35 and 36

— stop when required to do so by a police constable* in uniform;

RTA 1988 Sect 163

— stop when signalled to do so by a School Crossing Patrol exhibiting a 'STOP – CHILDREN' sign;

RTRA Sect 28

— see that your front and rear position lamps and rear registration plate lamps are lit at night;

RVLR No 24
RV(R and L)R

— use your headlamps at night in unlit areas;

RVLR No 25

— use your headlamps when visibility is seriously reduced, eg by thick fog.

RVLR No 25

You *must not*

— without reasonable excuse allow a child under 14 to travel in the front or rear of a vehicle to which the law applies unless suitably restrained;

RTA 1988 Sect 15
MV(WSBC)R 1982

— drive recklessly;

RTA 1988 Sect 2

— drive without due care and attention or without reasonable consideration for other persons using the road;

RTA 1988 Sect 3

— on the approach to an uncontrolled Zebra crossing or Pelican crossing marked by a pattern of zigzag lines, overtake the moving motor vehicle nearest to the crossing or the leading vehicle which has stopped to give way to a pedestrian on the crossing;

ZPCR No 10
PPCRGD No 19

— drive in a bus or cycle lane during its hours of operation;

RTRA Sects 1, 6 and 9

— wilfully drive on a footpath by the side of any road made or set apart for the use of foot passengers (E & W);

HA 1835 Sect 72

— drive along a footway or footpath (S);

R(S)A Sect 129(5)

— wilfully drive on a cycle track;

CTA Sect 2
R(S)A Sect 129(5)

— drive under the influence of drink or drugs;

RTA 1988 Sect 4(1)

— drive with a breath alcohol level higher than 35 µg/100 ml (equivalent to a blood alcohol level of 80 mg/100 ml);

RTA 1988 Sect 5

— drive your vehicle in reverse more than necessary;

CUR No 106

— drive a vehicle which emits excessive fumes and smoke;

CUR No 61

— drive a vehicle which has an unsuitable or defective silencer;

CUR No 54

* The reference to a police constable includes a traffic warden (Transport Act 1968).
† See the illustrations on page 126.

— drive a vehicle which cannot travel faster than 25 mph on a 70 mph dual carriageway without using an amber beacon;

RVLR No 17

— drive a vehicle in a manner which causes excessive and avoidable noise;

CUR No 97

— sound your horn at night (11.30 pm–7 am) in a built-up area;

CUR No 99

— carry passengers in such numbers or in such a manner as is likely to cause danger;

CUR No 100

— use four-way flashing hazard warning lamps when driving along except to warn others briefly if you have to slow quickly on a motorway or dual carriageway;

RVLR No 27

— switch on front or rear fog lamps unless visibility is *seriously* reduced;

RVLR No 27

— dazzle other road users with your headlamps or rear fog lamps.

RVLR No 27

When you stop you *must*

— set the brake and stop the engine before you leave the vehicle;

CUR No 107

— always switch off your headlamps and, at night, leave your front and rear position lamps and rear registration plate lamps on unless unlit parking is allowed;

RVLR Nos 27 and 24

— when required by the police, produce your driving licence, certificate of insurance and, if your vehicle is subject to compulsory testing, your test certificate, for examination. If necessary, you may instead produce them within seven days at any police station you select; in prescribed circumstances state your date of birth.

RTA 1988 Sects 164 and 165
RTPDA

You *must not*

— stop your vehicle in the Pelican controlled areas which are marked by a pattern of zigzag lines on either side of a Pelican crossing except to obey the signals, or in circumstances beyond your control, or

PPCRGD Nos 12, 13 and 14

when it is necessary to do so to avoid an accident, or to wait to turn right or left;

— stop your vehicle in the Zebra-controlled areas which are marked by a pattern of zigzag lines on either side of an uncontrolled Zebra crossing except to give precedence to a pedestrian on the crossing, or to wait to turn right or left, or in circumstances beyond your control, or when it is necessary to avoid an accident;

ZPCR No 12

— stop your vehicle within the limits of any type of pedestrian crossing except in circumstances beyond your control, or to avoid an accident;

PPCRGD Nos 12 and 13
ZPCR No 9

— park your vehicle or trailer on the road so as to cause unnecessary obstruction;

CUR No 103

— park in a bus or cycle lane during its hours of operation, except when permitted, to load or unload goods;

RTRA Sects 1, 6 and 9

— park your vehicle or trailer on the road in such a way that it is likely to cause danger to other road users;

RTA 1988 Sect 22

— park your vehicle on any length of road marked with double white lines even if one of the lines is broken;

RTA 1988 Sects 35 and 36
TSRGD 1981 No 23(2) (a)

— park on any verge, central reservation or footway, if your vehicle is a goods vehicle with a maximum laden weight exceeding 7.5 tonnes, except in certain circumstances, for example, if loading or unloading could only be performed there and the vehicle is not left unattended;

RTA 1988 Sect 19
HCVA 1973 Sect 2

— park at night on the right-hand side of the road (except in a one-way street);

CUR No 101

— park your vehicle on a cycle track;

CTA Sect 2
R(S)A Sect 129 (6)

— park your vehicle at night without lights unless: the road is subject to a speed limit of 30 mph or less; your vehicle is parked with its near side close to the kerb (unless it is in a one-way street or a recognised parking place); and no part of your vehicle is within 10 metres of a road junction;

RTRA Sects 1, 6, 9 and 53

— park your vehicle on common land more than 15 metres from a highway;

RTA 1988 Sect 34

— sound your horn while stationary, except in times of danger due to another moving vehicle nearby;

CUR No 99

— open any door of your vehicle so as to cause injury or danger to anyone.

CUR No 105

IF YOU ARE INVOLVED IN AN ACCIDENT

— which causes damage or injury to any other person, or other vehicle, or any animal (horse, cattle, ass, mule, sheep, pig, goat or dog) not in your vehicle, or roadside property:

RTA 1988 Sect 170

You *must*

— stop;

— give your own and the vehicle owner's name and address and the registration mark of the vehicle to anyone having reasonable grounds for requiring them;

— if you do not give your name and address to any such person at the time, report the accident to the police as soon as reasonably practicable, and in any case within 24 hours;

— if anyone is injured and you do not produce your certificate of insurance at the time to the police or to anyone who has with reasonable grounds required its production, report the accident to the police as soon as possible, and in any case within 24 hours, and either produce your certificate of insurance to the police when reporting the accident or ensure that it is produced within seven days thereafter at any police station you select.

TO DRIVERS, FRONT SEAT PASSENGERS AND REAR SEAT CHILD PASSENGERS

You *must*

— wear an approved type of seat belt or child restraint where required by law unless you are exempt from so doing.

MV(WSBCRS) 1989
MV(WSBC)R 1982
MV(WSB)R 1982
RTA 1988 Sects 14 and 15
MV(WSBCRS)R 1989

TO MOTORCYCLISTS AND MOPED RIDERS

Most of the requirements of the law relating to motor drivers, including those relating to pedestrian crossings, apply to you. In addition:

You *must*

— wear an approved type of safety helmet on all journeys;

MC(PH)R

— ensure that your exhaust system and silencer are of an approved type.

CUR 57

You *must not*

— carry more than one passenger on a two-wheeled machine, and the passenger must sit astride the cycle on a proper seat securely fitted behind the driver's seat and with proper rests for the feet;

RTA 1988 Sect 23
CUR No 102

— park in a parking meter zone except in a specially marked motorcycle park or, where not prohibited by a local order, at a meter.

RTRA Sect 53

TO PILLION PASSENGERS

You *must*

— wear an approved type of safety helmet whenever you ride as pillion passenger.

MC(PH)R

MOTORWAY DRIVING

General
Pedestrians, learner drivers, pedal cycles, motorcycles under 50 cc capacity, invalid carriages not exceeding 5 cwt unladen weight, certain slow-moving vehicles carrying oversized loads (except by special permission), agricultural vehicles and animals must not use motorways.

HA 1980 Sects 16 and 17 and Sch 4
MT(E&W)R Nos 4 and 11
R(S)A Sects 7 and 8
MT(S)R No 10

TO DRIVERS AND MOTORCYCLISTS

You *must*

— drive on the carriageways only;

MT(E&W)R No 5
MT(S)R No 4

— observe one-way driving on the carriageways;

MT(E&W)R No 6
MT(S)R No 5

— keep any animals in your charge in the vehicle or (in emergency) under proper control on the verge;

MT(E&W)R No 14
MTT(S)R No 12

— observe speed limits or any special speed for your vehicle;

RTRA Sect 17
RTRA Sect 86 and Sch 6

— observe flashing red signals when displayed over your lane or when displayed at the side of the carriageway (for example, on a slip road).

RTA 1988 Sect 36
TSRGD 1981 No 34(4)

You *must not*

— use a motorway if you are a learner (except heavy goods vehicle drivers);

MT(E&W)R No 11
MT(S)R No 10

— exceed 70 mph at any time;

MT(SL)R

— reverse on the carriageways;

MT(E&W)R No 8
MT(S)R No 7

— stop on the carriageways;

MT(E&W)R No 7(1)
MT(S)R No 6(1)

— stop on the hard shoulder except in an emergency;

MT(E&W)R No 9
MT(S)R No 8

— stop on the central reservation or verge;

MT(E&W)R No 10
MT(S)R No 9

— walk on the carriageway or on the central reservation except in an emergency;

MT(E&W)R No 13
MT(S)R No 11

— if you are driving a goods vehicle which has an operating weight of more than 7.5 tonnes, or any vehicle drawing a trailer, or a bus longer than 12 metres – use the right-hand lane of a motorway with three or more lanes except in exceptional circumstances as prescribed.

MT(E&W)R No 12
MT(E&W)(A)R
MT(S)R No 10A

FIRST AID ON THE ROAD

For those with no first aid training.

DANGER – Deal with threatened danger or you and the casualties may be killed. FURTHER COLLISIONS and FIRE are the dangers in a road accident.

Action: If possible warn other traffic. Switch off the engine. Impose a 'No Smoking' ban.

Obtaining further help: Send a bystander to call an ambulance as soon as possible; state the exact location of the accident and the numbers of vehicles and casualties involved.

People remaining in vehicles: Casualties remaining in vehicles should not be moved unless further danger is threatened.

If breathing has stopped: Remove any obvious obstruction in the mouth. Keep the head tilted backwards as far as possible – breathing may begin and the colour may improve. If not, pinch the casualty's nostrils together and blow into the mouth until the chest rises; withdraw, then repeat regularly once every four seconds until the casualty can breathe unaided.

If unconscious and breathing: Movement may further damage an injured back, so only move if in danger. If breathing becomes difficult or stops, treat as in foregoing paragraph.

If bleeding is present: Apply firm hand pressure over the wound, preferably using some clean material, without pressing on any foreign body in the wound. Secure a pad with a bandage or length of cloth. Raise limb to lessen the bleeding, providing it is not broken.

Reassurance: The casualty may be shocked but prompt treatment will minimise this; reassure him confidently; avoid unnecessary movement; keep him comfortable and prevent him getting cold; ensure he is not left alone.

Give the casualty NOTHING to drink.

Carry a first aid kit. Learn first aid – from the St John Ambulance Association and Brigade, St Andrew's Ambulance Association or the British Red Cross Society.

VEHICLE SECURITY

Over 1.5 million cars are broken into or stolen each year. That's one every 20 seconds. If you regularly park your car in a city street you have a one-in-four chance each year of having your car or its contents stolen.

A stolen car can mean having to walk back home late at night. It can mean weeks of delay sorting out insurance, extra expense getting into work, loss of personal possessions, and losing your no-claims bonus.

So when you leave your vehicle, always:
— Remove the ignition key and engage the steering lock.
— Lock the car.
— Close the windows *completely* – even the smallest gap is asking for trouble. But *never* leave children or pets in an unventilated car.
— Take any valuables with you, or lock them in the boot. Never leave vehicle documents in the car.
— At night, park in a well-lit place.

For extra security fit an anti-theft device such as an alarm or immobiliser. If you are buying a new car it's a good idea to check the level of built-in security features. And it's well worth while having your registration number etched on all your car windows. This is a cheap and effective deterrent to professional thieves.